RAISE

THE

WHITE FLAG

Donald P. Journeaux

A study through one pair of eyes

of the Occupation of Jersey

by German forces 1940 to 1945

ASHFORD, BUCHAN & ENRIGHT
LEATHERHEAD

Published in 1995 by Ashford, Buchan & Enright
(which is an imprint of Natural Magic Ltd.)
Leatherhead, Surrey KT24 5HH

British Library Cataloguing in Publication Data

ISBN 1 85253 321 8

Cover design by Peter Easley

Designed and typeset by Priory Publications
Haywards Heath, West Sussex

Printed by FotoDirect Ltd
Brighton, East Sussex

Raise the White Flag

Donald P. Journeaux

For Irene

for our wonderful life together

ACKNOWLEDGEMENTS

I offer my most grateful thanks to all of those who gave me assistance, in various ways, in the preparation of this book.

I would particularly like to mention Mrs Cecil Journeaux, my sister-in-law, for her impressive and unfaltering help towards the completion of this book; Mrs Dennis Nursey for her constant and stimulating encouragement; Mrs Jim Scriven for her efforts in procuring photographs; and to the members of staff of the *Jersey Evening Post* for their unfailing assistance.

My sincere thanks to Mr John Hibbs, Headmaster of Victoria College Preparatory School, for so kindly writing the Preface; and my thanks too to Mr Nigel Whitnall, editor, and Mr John Mole and staff of Ashford, Buchan & Enright for their tremendous effort in publishing the book in such a short time.

PREFACE

For thousands of years the Channel Island of Jersey has been an insignificant backwater off the coast of France where, apart from a few periods when the island has become a player on the world stage, things have gone on year by year and century by century with little change. Although the young children of my generation did not realise it at the time, we lived through the darkest days of island history since the Viking invasions more than a thousand years ago.

For those of my parents' generation, the fear and deprivation of those five years were something to be swept away and forgotten like an unhappy nightmare but for us there were aspects of those years which made it a less frightening time to grow up – there was little traffic and none of the dangers of an overcrowded island to fence us in, no television or long hours of school work to inhibit our play.

Donald Journeaux was an honorary uncle to my sister and me and he brought bright moments to what were long grey days. The dance and acting school at the Studio in New Street took us off the streets and gave us experience and memories of the real theatre which have been with us for the rest of our lives. The demand for entertainment meant that Donald's shows at the Opera House, which were great successes, enabled people to develop talents which in normal times would not have had a chance to be expressed.

Many of my brightest memories of those years are associated with Donald and Irene. The shows of course, but also our evacuation to Donald's farm in the summer of 1940, where we arrived just evading the curfew time of 9.00 p.m. and where I spent the most idyllic summer of my life as a five year old, climbing trees, looking after calves, and playing in the tomato fields.

Donald's memoirs have brought back those days of fifty years ago, the good times but also the dark ones when one could be shot, imprisoned or deported at the whim of the occupying power. The courage of people like Donald and Irene gives the lie to those who wish to brand the occupied islanders as traitors. Had we known what barbaric crimes were being committed in Europe we might have been even more fearful than we were.

John Hibbs
Headmaster
Victoria Preparatory School
St Helier
January 1995

Jersey

Plémont

Corbière

St. Ouens
Bay

St. Brelade's
Bay

Portelet Bay

Harbour

Harve-Despas

St. Ouens
Manor ●

Airport ●

Portelet ●

Noirmont

St. Helier

St. Lawrence

German
Underground
Hospital ●

St. Aubin's
Bay

Grand Vaux ●

Houge Bie ●

St. Saviour ●
Palace Hotel

Five Oaks ●

St.
Clement's
Bay

La Rocque

St. John's

St. Martin's

Golf
Course

Our House ●

Fauvic

Grouville
Bay

Faldouet

St.
Catherine's
Bay

Harbour

Gorey

Rozel Bay

CHAPTER ONE

THE EARLY DAYS

Before I start on the days and years of the Occupation, there are a few things that I should disclose about myself.

During the 1930s I owned a small farm with a lovely old house, one horse, one cow, a tractor and a lorry, and I employed one person, growing mainly potato and tomato crops.

My main interest, however, had always been with the performing arts and my love of music was very strong. Early on I had had lessons in singing and various dance forms. I had joined the Jersey Green Room Club, an amateur dramatic society, and I had performed in many of their productions, as well as doing the choreography for their musicals. Whenever the Denville Players, a professional English repertory company, made one of their frequent visits to Jersey I was able to take part in some of their plays. In fact, they asked me if I would like to join the company. I was not able to do so then, but this was certainly an encouraging offer.

In 1937 I was delighted to be asked to help put on an evening performance to follow the annual 'Battle of Flowers' parade. Having given much thought to this exciting project, I decided to present *The Blue Danube* with a chorus of about forty male singers and ninety dancers. It was an enormous undertaking for an amateur. Apart from arranging the choreography, I also had to go to London to the well-known costumers Simmonds & Co to select costumes. You can see that the creative side of my life was gradually taking over by the time that war broke out.

I married Irene Newland in January 1940. It was not a good start to our married life: during the months following, as news of the war became more grave and the Battle of Dunkirk and subsequent occupation of France ensued, I was still recuperating from an operation and so we were unable to leave Jersey to join the war effort.

On June 19th 1940 the British Government declared the Channel Islands a Demilitarised Zone and on the 20th an evacuation took place.

My wife and I joined the queues for the few boats that were available. There was widespread confusion and many who queued did not get away, while others somehow bypassed the waiting and got onto the boats.

Everyone was bewildered. People were going around visiting friends and family and trying to decide what was best, and constantly changing their minds, so that when about 14,000 people did leave the Island, houses were abandoned, cars left stranded on the pier and, in some cases, cattle were left unmilked in the fields.

Eventually, Irene and I decided that we should stay in Jersey. My father-in-law, M.H.Newland, was a sick man and would not have survived the journey on a coal boat, which seemed to be the only thing available. We felt we should not leave him.

On June 28th Jersey suffered its first surprise attack when three German planes swept screaming in very low over the sea from the French coast. A friend of mine, Bertram Payn, was outside with his mother at La Rocque when the first bombs were dropped. It was a terrifying experience for them and a miracle that they were not killed. Two bombs fell, one on the water without exploding, and the other on the slipway. The shrapnel caused a vast amount of damage to the cottages nearby, and all the windows in the village were shattered.

Altogether three people were killed and quite a number wounded. It was not possible at that point to get an ambulance as they were all busy in the town. Bertram, assisted by friends, had the painful duty of wrapping the bodies in tarpaulin and lifting them into a lorry. Fortunately a delivery van came to his rescue and the bodies were transferred into it and taken to hospital.

It had all happened in such a short space of time, but it had a lasting effect on the villagers. After that when planes came over they would run to hide in the channel of the dried-up brook behind the houses.

Meanwhile the planes had wreaked havoc in St Helier. Bombs had been dropped in the harbour, damaging many small boats and setting light to nearby stores. The Yacht Hotel and other buildings suffered and many windows were smashed including some of the stained-glass windows in St Helier's Church.

On Mount Bingham the roof of a friend's house was hit, and in a house across the road a man was killed. Bombs also fell on Fort Regent. Ten people were killed and a number injured, mainly by shrapnel. It was fortuntate that there wasn't greater loss of life, although the Germans may have considered the raid a failure. Perhaps the main aim was to frighten people.

On July 1st a communique from the Commander of the German Forces in Normandy, addressed to the Governor of the Island, was dropped from a plane, ordering white crosses to be placed in the centre of the airport and in the inner basin of the harbour. Buildings, fortifications and houses were each to show a white flag and all these things were to be in place by 7am on July 2nd and to

BAILIFF ADDRESSES CROWD IN SQUARE

"KEEP CALM AND OBEY ORDERS"

"GOD'S BLESSING UPON YOU ALL"

A large crowd gathered in the Royal Square from an early hour and the centre of the square was roped off to allow of the stipulated white cross to be painted in the centre. Another cross was painted on the car park on the Weighbridge.

About 12.30 the Bailiff of Jersey, obviously deeply affected, appeared on the Royal Court steps and addressed the crowd through the amplifier installation.

He told the public, speaking with emotion, how, early this morning, three identical copies of a proclamation addressed to the Military and Civil Governor of the Island had been handed to him after having been dropped from aircraft and that he had made as accurate a translation as it was possible to get. The Bailiff then read the proclamation, which was signed by the Governor of the German Air Forces in Normandy, and which called for the immediate and peaceful surrender of the military establishments and the whole Island under pain of bombardment, as set out herewith.

After reading the proclamation the Bailiff appealed to the public to remain calm, and stressed the danger to all which might be caused by anyone disobeying orders given by the occupying forces. "We shall be under occupation," he said, "and under such circumstances I appeal to you all to remain calm and to do nothing which would invite repressive measures." He pointed out with emphasis that to cause trouble meant that measures might be taken against the whole population.

The Bailiff also announced that places of amusement would remain open to-night and that no curfew would be imposed but that all licences of any kind for the sale of any sort of intoxicants were withdrawn and he appealed to all who had not done so to give up any arms which they might still possess, as the possession of arms was dangerous at such a time.

The Bailiff also laid great emphasis on the final paragraph of the German note, which states very definitely that in the event of peaceful surrender the lives, properties and liberties of the population of the island would be safeguarded.

"There will be no curfew to-night," he said, "but I hope that you will, as I hope to be able to do, remain quietly in your own homes to-night. I do not know when I shall have the opportunity of speaking to you again, but until then I pray God's Blessing upon you all."

The crowd then dispersed in an orderly manner.

remain there until the occupation of the Island by German troops was completed.

A notice in the *Jersey Evening Post*, the Island's daily newspaper, informed us that inhabitants had to be indoors from 11pm until 5am; no spirits were to be supplied or obtained or consumed (although this did not apply to private houses); the sale of motor spirit was prohibited, except for essential services; the use of private cars was forbidden; it was also forbidden to listen to any transmitting station; and all firearms were to be delivered to the Town Hall. This was signed by Kommandant Cussack. We wondered how many people would obey the last order.

Like many others, Irene and I suffered greatly that evening. We felt humiliated at having to hang out a white flag. Nothing could be more abhorrent to us, but we knew that it had to be done. Everyone had to comply as you could not put others at risk by ignoring such an order. With a feeling of hopelessness I found an old torn cloth (I could make that small gesture of defiance), attached it to a stake and fixed it to the chimney pot.

After a sleepless night, we went over to Irene's parents' home. The gardener had put up their white flag – and so they had not even been obliged to see it, thereby at least saving them some trauma.

Everything seemed strange. We felt so agitated. Something needed to be done, but we did not know what. How could we possibly make any plans? Everything everywhere was confusion.

The occupation of the Island was carried out efficiently and in an orderly fashion. Shortly after the order to display white flags, which had been given by the Commander of the German Air Force in Normandy, German troops landed at Jersey Airport. Guards were at once posted at the Post Office and Telephone Exchange, and soldiers were billeted in hotels.

Very soon it became known that money would be devalued. Local people and even the German troops were descending on the shops and I decided I should have to join them and bring in some of the many things we should require. Tea, coffee, tins of meat, sugar, rice, candles and matches, medicines...what did we need? It was so difficult to make up one's mind. We had nothing to go by and felt as though we had been thrown in at the deep end.

The town was packed with people and soldiers. The soldiers looked happy, no doubt because they were, for a time at least, away from the fighting. The sensation of strangeness continued. I felt as though I were in a comic opera! Time, of course, would change that.

I was glad that I had my old bicycle. The shops had soon sold out of cycles and people who had them were being offered double the price of a new one. I would not part with mine, because we lived about three miles from St Helier and we needed to be able to get about.

I went out again the following day to try to collect a few more essential items. I was worried as to whether I was indeed doing the right thing because there would be people without enough money to lay in a store of any kind. It was not a happy thought, but the Germans were buying, so one felt one was not doing any harm. I foresaw that all would very soon be on ration.

We spent a great deal of time at 'Terra Nova', the home of my in-laws, as we both had cycles. We were eager to be together and tried to make plans for our immediate future.

I had three chicken runs and I thought that if I obtained some rabbits I could keep them in the runs on the lawn. Not only would they keep the grass down, but they would be easy to take care of and they would provide some good meals in the future. So Irene and I spent all the following day trying to buy rabbits from various farms. It was just as well that we started at once, because later it became very difficult to get any. We managed to collect seven and we

Germany officers at Jersey Airport, met by the Bailiff, Alexander Cautanche, second left.
(Photo courtesy Jersey Evening Post)

hoped that they would get busy and reproduce.

I had a wire-haired terrier named Timmy, a lovely little dog, who came with me everywhere. In former times he had been used to catching wild rabbits, but he understood that these rabbits were different, because he watched me feed them and stroke them. One day, he decided that it would be fun to play with them. He managed to push the hutch away from the run and in no time he was rushing around with them all over the place. When I discovered him and reprimanded him, he helped me to coax them back into their run, just like a sheep dog.

German currency in use on the Islands

Timmy was highly intelligent and sometimes, when we left him at home, he was able to get out of the kitchen window and would make the rounds of our various friends until he found us.

More and more Germans arrived on the Island and were billeted in various hotels. At that time the Kommandant and his officers were being very courteous and tried to fraternise. The position was very difficult for the Bailiff and various officials as they had to be in touch constantly, and very soon orders started to appear in the *Evening Post*, most of them signed by both Kommandant Cussack and the Bailiff, A.M.Coutanche.

One morning, shortly after the Germans had arrived on the Island, planes flew low over my farm. With the memory of the attack on La Rocque still fresh in their minds, the men working in the tomato field threw themselves on the ground. Luckily no-one was hurt on this occasion. Later on, after I had disposed of the farm, a gun emplacement was mounted on one of the fields.

The first rations were, per person per week: butter 4oz, sugar 4oz, meat 3/4lb (including bone and fat), tea 4oz. Application could be made for a ration of paraffin. Unfortunately we did not have more than one stove and two lamps between us. Other things were unrationed at this time, and some prices were: potatoes 5s per cwt, tomatoes 2d per lb. This may look very little until you consider that a labourer's wage was 36 shillings (£1.80 in today's currency) per week.

German currency was now in circulation, with seven marks to the pound sterling. Care had to be taken as counterfeit marks had been identified.

Later on the Jersey authorities also issued a penny stamp, a unique first for the Island.

The mail service was again linked up with Guernsey and eleven passengers who had been caught there at the time of the invasion were returned to Jersey. Each day the *Evening Post* published articles in both English and German. Soon after the newspaper became subject to censorship.

Censorship at the Jersey Evening Post with German officers and the editor, Mr Arthur Harrison.
(Photo courtesy Jersey Evening Post)

The Old Victorians Sports Club had a meeting and decided that we should try to contact any playing members on the Island to arrange a cricket match. I was elected Honorary Treasurer and I had to collect two shillings and six pence from every member. This may seem odd in the circumstances in which we found ourselves, but we believed it was important to keep up as normal a life as possible. A boost to morale was highly desirable and we thought we should make that effort whenever we could.

As lights were no longer allowed to be used in churches in order to save electricity, services were now being conducted in the afternoon. But one evening the Germans held a recital for their troops in one of the churches, thereby disobeying their own orders! Periodically German chaplains would take the services at the Roman Catholic churches at St Helier, St Peter and St Mary.

The Germans ran an electric cable to one of the dairies to provide power for milk pasteurisation. As the machinery had not been in operation for some time large quantities of milk had gone sour.

One strange order circulated concerned pigeons. The Germans had been searching for them and destroying them, much to the disgust of people known to us who kept them.

The States of Jersey ordered that a 1940 Census should take place, no doubt to ascertain how many people had left the Island. There were already rumours that English people, as opposed to native Islanders, would be deported, which did, in fact, occur later on.

My thoughts at that time were constantly of trying to get away, but the undertaking was daunting. I had a canoe hidden in a hayloft, but I could not work out how to get it down to the shore without help. I could not involve anyone else, unless they also wished to get away. The attempt was pretty well out of the question.

On August 9th we had our first change of Kommandant. Cussack had been reasonable and we soon learnt that, as first Kommandant, he had hidden the iron hand in the velvet glove. Colonel Schumacher who replaced him we later discovered to be of a very different order.

We owned a bungalow on the dunes in Grouville Bay. Before the War the bay was lined with similar wooden buildings where people would spend the day or the weekend or even some weeks of the summer. Mostly they were larger than the beach huts we see in some seaside towns today, and some were comfortably furnished. We heard that these bungalows were being broken into and damaged and so we decided to have ours brought up to our own house, Greenacre, at Maufant.

By this time a thriving exchange system was in operation and goods were advertised in the 'Exchange and Mart' column of the *Evening Post.* Some of the items make amusing reading now: Rabbit for sugar or treacle; Wellingtons, size 12, for sugar; English ale for roasting turkey; Money for rabbits; Foodstuffs for cycle parts. There were many requests for shoes, especially for exchanging sizes – of increasing importance for growing children. In addition there was a vast variety of other items being offered in exchange for sugar.

Round about this time an order was given to the bakeries that bread should consist of 80 lb of flour to 20 lb of mashed potato.

The Jersey Green Room Club held its Annual General Meeting as if all were normal. I was happy to see that every effort would be made to continue, although quite a number of members had left the Island. I was once more elected to the Committee, and prepared to be an active member. It was difficult to predict just what we would be able to accomplish under the conditions, but we were determined to continue to entertain the public.

Forms for the registration of cars and lorries had to be filled in and returned by 21st September. Following this, the picture below appeared in the *Evening Post*, showing how a motor van had been converted into a horse-drawn vehicle.

Quite soon I was able to obtain a blue permit to go fishing. In my case, this meant low-water fishing, but small-boat fishing was also allowed from 6am to 8pm. However, fishing was completely prohibited later on, a great pity as I had started to go low-water fishing for limpets as food for my dog, or for sand-eels.

We had to obtain a doctor's certificate to get various items for my father-in-

(Photo courtesy Jersey Evening Post)

law Mr Newland, though not all were available. Later he was allowed extra milk, which was a great help.

The next blow was the collection of the Newlands' car. It was a 1940 model for which they received no compensation. Later I saw it in the town, loaded with German officers.

The Green Room Club at last took the plunge and produced *Scrapbook*, a 'Revue of Revues', compiled from shows dating back to 1928 and produced by Kenneth Britton. I was fortunate to be one of the company and to arrange some of the dances. It was staged at the Playhouse and the theatre was packed at each performance. I must say it felt good to be doing something that gave people pleasure.

Military zones were now being enlarged and anyone found within them during prohibited hours would be arrested. Patrols were ordered to shoot anyone who ignored their challenge. Shops were to be closed for ten days so that an inventory of soap, shoes and textiles could be made. The weekly allowance to civilians of cigarettes was twenty, plus 2oz of tobacco, but for the first time, German forces had to produce a permit for their daily ration of twenty cigarettes or 1oz of tobacco. Civilians making an application for their cigarette ration now had to produce their food ration books.

Some other amusing items from the Exchange and Mart section of the *Evening Post* included: One lady's cycle for doe ferret; Cockerel for 9 lb of candles; 1 Belgian doe hare in kindle for 120-volt battery; Violin (with bow) for hire, three shillings per week.

At this point I have to mention that our rabbits were all stolen one night. That was indeed sad news. It would mean saying goodbye to some good meals, and replacing them would now be impossible.

Soon after this the Island suffered its fiercest gale within living memory. Trees and telephone and electricity poles were uprooted; over 1,000 lines went down and there was tremendous damage throughout the Island. The velocity of the wind during the night between 9.30pm and 12.30am was more than 83 miles per hour and, as you may imagine, repairing essential services and military lines had priority.

Orders of all kinds were now being published thick and fast. The worst for us was the 'Registration of Male British Subjects'. Irene's father promptly took to his bed: in no way would he be able to get to the Parish Hall. Mr Billot, the Constable of the parish, said that it was impossible for Irene's father to do so as he was bedridden. We heard no more, but a lot of people were unlucky and were deported to concentration camps in Germany, although at this stage no-one realised what their fate there would be.

By October 25th wheat flour was rationed at 4oz per person per week and tea was reduced to 2oz. Anyone with a wireless transmitter was liable for the death penalty.

One afternoon a friendly neighbouring farmer knocked at the door and asked if we would like half a pig, and not at a black market price. We were delighted and quite overcome at his kindness in being willing to share his pig. It arrived later that day. There it was, lying on the kitchen table. We gazed in awe and savoured our fantastic piece of luck. I just had no idea how to carve it up but I did have a very good knife and my old scout axe could be brought into action on the bones.

But where was I to begin? Irene suggested that the trotters should be dealt with first, so a start was made, but it was only after quite some time and much effort that I was able to carve it up into fairly respectable sections.

I had only just completed the job when there was a knock at the door. Panic! We could not be caught with all that pork, so we hastily plunged most of it into the oven. While Irene went to the door I put the rest into saucepans and covered the mess on the table. It turned out to be two young German soldiers and Irene was certain that they were going to search the house, but they just wanted to buy our bicycles. They were very young and spoke little English. We had to explain that we could not manage without them as we had to cycle into town each day for rehearsals. They were quite polite, thanked us and went away.

We really thought that we had been subjected to enough excitement for one day. All was not over, however. As we did not intend to keep all the meat, I was obliged to go round to various friends with joints of pork. This was a bit risky as I could easily have been stopped and searched. Normally I carried rabbit food which I gathered from the hedges piled on top of my bicycle basket, and I thought this would be the best protection as it would look genuine. This subterfuge succeeded.

The next big worry was my car. I had not registered when the call came for 1939 cars as I could pretend that it was a 1938 model. But now something had to be done. I had no intention of presenting my car for sale. It was a Morris Coupe, a pretty car, pale grey with yellow leather seats. I was not prepared to suffer the humiliation of seeing Germans riding in it, so it must be hidden. An old shed was found, not too far away and well off the road. I drove it there instead of to the garage for German inspection, and it was hidden behind an old bus. I had the wheels removed, wrapped and buried some distance away. The poor car truly suffered an indignity and I longed for the day when I could bring her back again to her former glory.

Evidently the Field Command were worried about the possiblity of air-raids and issued notice of precautions to be enforced. Identity cards had to be carried at all times and there were to be no fires in the open air during the hours of darkness. Warnings were also issued that, as there were more and more troops on the Island, they might be billeted on people with large houses.

This made it imperative that we should give up our house and go to live with Irene's parents for the duration of the war. This, we hoped, would ensure that soldiers were not billeted on them and it would also be easier to manage our food.

About this time Irene and I reluctantly came to the conclusion that we should avoid having children. As time went by, what with the lack of food, heat and other things, we realised we had made the right decision.

CHAPTER TWO

JOINING FORCES

Irene's father was not any better. We knew of a couple living in town who were eager to get out into the country, so I made contact with them. They moved into our house and everyone was satisfied with the arrangements. I got permission to obtain transport for the removal and all was soon accomplished.

The Newlands' car was gone and so we were able to store furniture in the garage. We celebrated that night with a slice of the famous pig. Irene's parents now felt more comfortable with us joining them, but at the back of all our minds was the question, 'How long? How long?'

Many items were already in short supply. The Department of Labour urgently required boots and shoes from anyone who was willing to give or sell to the States. Children, of course, were growing and would soon need larger sizes.

The radio news from England was not good. We listened every day and we dreaded the time when wirelesses would have to be handed in. We could think of few worse things than to be without the news. An order had already been made, but it had been postponed for the time being.

Things were steadily getting tighter, with a flood of new orders appearing in the *Evening Post*. Some of these concerned 'Protection against pillage', 'The hoarding of silver', 'The supply of petrol to a reduced bus service'. Postal communication between the Island and Occupied French Territory, Italy and Belgium was permitted, if one could get a letter onto one of the barges going to France.

Landmines had been laid on the foreshore of the Island. We hated to see the barbed wire and the notices showing a skull and crossbones and the words 'Achtung! Minen!' Areas of Grouville Common and other open spaces were also mined and were highly dangerous.

Some of the orders were more irritating than serious, as when everyone had to register again by 24th January 1941, only two months after the original Census, or having to fill in forms as to one's consumption of milk and the name of one's retailer. On January 8th 1941 the curfew was changed. It now lasted from 10pm to 6am in St Helier and 9pm to 6am in all other parishes. This made it pretty difficult to get home after rehearsals.

Then, what we had dreaded overtook us. The decree of the Feld Kommandant, registered in the Royal Court, ordered the confiscation, and placing in safe custody, of all Wireless Receiving Sets of the Civil Population. The dates of the delivery of the sets were to be notified in due course. No doubt we would have a few days in hand, but no matter, all four of us had only one thing in mind: only three of the four sets we had between us would go and the one with the best battery would remain. It was a chance that had to be taken. Although we got a certain amount of news from the *Evening Post*, this was, as I have said, censored, and in any case, to us the voice of the BBC was essential. It was what we waited for all day, the Nine O'Clock News, with perhaps the voice of Winston Churchill. Unfortunately at this stage it was mostly bad news (and this had a keenly depressing effect on the population which you could almost touch). But we still wanted to know.

We had planned to dig a hole under a very large pine tree which would, when the time came, be the hideaway. Masses of pine needles could be used to cover the spot and the branches came right down to the ground. I found a box just the right size to accommodate our precious wireless set which we would wrap in an old piece of tarpaulin in order to keep it absolutely dry. The only problem would be bringing it in and out of the house, as that would be my job and I could not always be home by 9pm.

Coffee substitute was available, made from roasted corn, which was considered by doctors to be more wholesome than coffee or tea. I do not think that supplies lasted very long. Eventually we were obliged to make our own tea from blackberry leaves and coffee from grated sugarbeet.

It was announced that the Feld Kommandant and his Kriegsverwaltungsrat [war council], in co-operation with the Island authorities, intended to make the Islands self-sufficient. A good plan but, we thought, beset with untold difficulties. However, representatives from both Jersey and Guernsey were taken over to the French port of Granville to buy what was needed. They were permitted to travel all over France in cars put at their disposal by the German military authorities. They contracted to buy 6,000 tons of flour. Meat was purchased in the Department of La Manche, slaughtered in Granville and the carcasses brought to the Islands. Fortunately, there were still German boats and barges able to make the crossing. I would have liked to have spoken to our representative about the conditions he must have seen in France and to find out whether he had been able to speak to people.

We hoped that we would be able to export potatoes as they were required in many parts of France, and this would bring in money for the goods we required. Later large stocks of coal were purchased but transportation proved difficult. The public were asked to economise by using potatoes instead of bread. At this point 1lb loaves were 2d each.

A list of news from relatives abroad was published, but sadly there was nothing for us. Months later we at last received a Red Cross message from my brother Cecil. It contained no news, but we were very glad just to know that he was alive and well. In that same batch of messages, two other friends were mentioned and two boys who had been in my year at school.

Several people were arrested for being out after curfew, and even for cycling two abreast. A man was challenged by soldiers when he was seen walking in the military zone. He started to run and the soldiers shouted, 'Halt!' He ignored the command and was shot dead.

Minor restrictions continued to multiply and life became more bewildering as time went on. Telephone calls must not exceed three minutes. To buy meat one had to register with a butcher and give him one's name and address. With each purchase he had to take the coupons from the book and sign the counterfoil. Part of the ration could be in the form of meat stew which became obtainable in glass containers. It was still possible to eat in a restaurant or hotel, but ration books had to be produced and coupons used. Prices were fixed for all food.

Here follows a little more humour from the *Evening Post* 'Exchange and Mart' section (my father-in-law took great delight in reading out this section regularly): Piano for bed or wardrobe; Pram for lady's cycle; Drake for duck; Lady's wellingtons for large saucepan.

We ourselves did not have much to exchange, although I eventually traded my riding boots for tea. This was done privately and was for us a very important transaction as we had run out of proper tea, having to resort to tea substitute, which was awful!

The following recipe, also from the *Evening Post*, gives an idea of the food situation at the time. Potato Milk Pudding: 1lb potatoes, 1½ pints cold water, 1 pint milk, ½ teaspoon salt, 1½ tablespoons sugar, vanilla or almond essence. This can be served with baked apples. Needless to say, we did not sample it!

The number of troops here continued to ebb and flow. A great number came to the Island either to train or to rest. When they first arrived, many of them, seeing the names King Street, Queen Street and Charing Cross, became quite excited and sent messages home saying they were in London.

Now back to the theatre. Kenneth Britton and Richard Winnerah presented the marvellous play *The Light of Heart* by Emlyn Williams. It was an excellent production. They gathered a first-class cast from the Green Room Club, all of whom portrayed their parts splendidly, despite the difficult requirement for all parts to be spoken in a Welsh accent. I was glad to be acting as stage manager for the first time.

Sadly there was a disastrous fire at St Ouen's Manor, which was being occupied by German soldiers. It was one of Jersey's most beautiful houses and ancestral home of the de Carteret family who had lived there for generations and who had been among the leading Seigneurs of the Island since the tenth century. Their history had been bound up with that of Jersey, and much treasure was lost when the drawing room, with many valuable portraits of past de Carterets, and the west wing, the oldest part of the building, were completely gutted.

This incident reminded Irene and I that we were breaking the law for when we moved into the Newlands' home we had stored many items in their loft including some inflammable material.

By the end of March 1941 we had reached the stage when coal and electricity were not allowed to be used for heating. If any person contravened this order they were liable to imprisonment and a fine. This made it very difficult to cook and keep the house warm. The only answer was to burn wood in the open fireplace. Fortunately we had a good supply for the moment, but how long would it have to last?

We were glad that we had moved in with the Newlands as another order was issued about the billeting of soldiers. It was necessary, for military reasons, to make provision for accommodation at short notice for the Army of Occupation. More troops were to arrive on the Island and this would mean that even more Germans would be eating up our food.

Boats on shore or in garages had to be brought to the harbours although, on the recommendation of the States, fishermen already holding permits were to be allowed out within a three-mile limit from St Helier, St Aubin, La Rocque, Gorey and Rozel Bay. They had to return before dark or if it became at all misty. Any wireless transmitter on board a boat had to be dismantled and a white flag flown.

We were sad to hear that an old friend of the family, Colonel W.A.Stocker of St Martin, was knocked down by a car in Hill Street and later died in hospital. It seemed clear that the car was not driven by a Jerseyman as no driver's name was mentioned.

Colonel Stocker and I had both been in the choir of St Martin's Church. When as a young boy I used to sing solos he would insist that I stand in the aisle so that my voice would carry better. He was great fun and had many stories to tell, and was also President of the Island's Football Club.

Mr C.W.Mackon was also involved in a fatal accident. Cycling down the road he collided with a German car: the German jury returned a most unsatisfactory verdict of 'death from acute heart failure following a terrible accident in which he sustained head injuries'.

One-way traffic regulations in Columbrie were suspended following the accident. Surprisingly the Germans admitted that their personnel had been the principal offenders. There was no doubt that they were dangerous drivers, constantly being involved in bad accidents.

One piece of good news was that a workshop was established to turn old boots and shoes into clogs. We were urged to save old footwear so that wooden soles and heels could be fitted. The finished products were put on display in the St Helier shops.

And now to the theatre once again. Kenneth Britton and Richard Winnerah presented *Tonight at 8.30*, a group of six one-act plays by Noel Coward. On this occasion the following three were performed: *Hands across the Sea, Fumed Oak* and *Ways and Means*. The cast was more or less the same as in the previous production, although this time I was not stage manager but had parts in two of the plays.

Finding rehearsal rooms was a problem but Mrs Venn of the Royal Hotel kindly came to our rescue. A nice touch was provided by Graeme Bentlif who played a selection of Noel Coward's music during the intervals. We felt that, in view of the curfew, the title of the production should have been changed to *Tonight at 7.15!*

Motor vehicles down to 1935 were now having to be brought in, even those which had previously been rejected. Fuel for driving them to the collection point was to be provided without charge. From June 1st 1941 we were ordered to drive on the right.

Prices of different types of fish were controlled, and I remember shelled lobsters being listed as 1s 8d per pint. They never came our way, at any price! We were able to get spider crabs and mackerel from Gorey Harbour on one or two occasions. I believe that the Germans took a good proportion for themselves, and there were many days when the fishermen were not allowed out. About this time we had to apply for new ration books and re-register with a butcher.

It was prohibited, without written permission, to cut down any standing tree or cut up any felled or fallen tree. One could buy wood blocks at 65s a ton, if one could find them. No wonder that trees continued to disappear from the scene.

On October 17th 1941 the Germans took over Woolworth's, indiscriminately smashing the counters and fittings. They also commandeered the Co-operative Wholesale Society bakery, the sports stadium and many more houses on Mont Felard and David Place. The Kommandant took College House for himself.

The Germans declared that the Island was going to become as well fortified as Gibraltar. Artillery practice continued constantly, as they expected that the British would attempt to recapture the Island. That would be the day! They had imported vast stores and work of every description was underway. Large tunnels were being dug in various parts of the Island.

At short notice the military sought a supply of furniture and household effects for the use of the Army of Occupation. They required a full list from the authorities of goods belonging to absent people. The Kommandant was now Graf von Schmettow.

When Messrs Britton and Winnerah decided to present *Sally*, a musical which had been produced at Springfield Hall, St Helier, some years before, I was lucky enough to be in the cast and to be asked to arrange the dances. It appeared that I had to obtain a teaching permit from the Feld Kommandant. It was forwarded for approval to the Island authorities and was signed and forwarded to me with approval by A.M. Coutanche. The stupid part of this was that the permit mentioned 'Instruction in dancing on Friday evenings'. To do this show I would require much more time than that!

I had been thinking for some time that I would like to be able to do something for the younger age group as there was very little for their amusement, and while we were working on this show they persuaded me to start a theatre school. I spent a great deal of time searching for a suitable place which I eventually found in St Helier. My heart sank when I realised that I would have to apply yet again for more permits but, much to my delight, they actually arrived in time for an announcement of the opening to be placed in the programme for *Sally*.

I finally had No 31, New Street ready for interviews, which were to be held on 12th and 13th September. It was a good suite of rooms, having two large studios with wood floors, together with a dressing room and the usual amenities. We offered classes for young people and adults in Ballet, Elocution and Musical Comedy, and special classes for children. When we opened on September 22nd, although teachers for some of the classes were still to be appointed, I felt that we were off to a good start. All would be under my personal supervision and we had 17 pupils and the promise of more to join in the following weeks. I was glad that I had launched out on this enterprise and I hoped that it would boost the morale of everyone involved.

From time to time we were reminded of the very serious side of life under enemy occupation. An order was published entitled 'Protection against acts of sabotage'. It was an offence to hide or shelter prisoners of war or persons belonging to the armed forces of the enemy, for example, the crew of an aircraft which had made a forced landing. This offence was punishable by death.

Despite this warning, a good friend of ours hid and fed a Russian who had escaped from the Germans for quite some time. In fact there were three families involved and they passed him from one to another, a very dangerous act of compassion. Eventually he had to move away and we had no further news of him.

My father, Charles P. Journeaux, received a Red Cross message from his cousin in Southampton that my brother was well and in Africa. That was indeed good news. Several people that I knew were mentioned in that same batch of messages. It would have been lovely to be able to correspond freely. I just wished that I too was off this island.

Rations now included 10 1/2 oz of bread per week, but only 1oz of tea. From 'Exchange and Mart': Poultry for ferret; Doe rabbit with seven young for foodstuff and candles; 1lb rhubarb for three candles; 1lb blackberries for 1 dozen candles; Whisky, gin or cognac for baby's high chair; Pram canopy for silk stockings.

On September 21st 1941 Dennis Vibert, a young Jerseyman, made two attempts to escape from the Island. The first failed as he ran into stormy weather and was obliged to turn back. He was most fortunate not to be discovered.

With the second attempt he also ran into problems. The outboard engine on his craft fell into the sea and he had to row for two days without food, eventually covering 150 miles. He was finally picked up by HMS *Brocklesby* which took him to Dartmouth. It was a fantastic solo performance.

A warning from the Feld Kommandant was given to the Bailiff at this time that a number of civilians had been seen loitering in the neighbourhood of Fort Regent. When the military patrol approached the civilians, they had thrown down a gun of amateur construction and had run away. Besides this, signposts had been altered, and 'V' (for Victory) signs painted on houses and walls. Three offenders were sentenced to nine months' imprisonment each.

We never found out what happened to all the flour that had been bought in France, but an amendment was later made to the rationing provisions. Male civilians born on or before December 31st 1931 were to receive 4lb of bread, male manual workers 6lb. Persons born on or after January 1st 1932, male or female, would receive 1lb. A 4oz ration of semolina would now cost 4d. The issue of pipe tobacco was suspended and cigarettes were reduced to ten per week.

The buildings of both Victoria College Boys School and the Jersey Ladies College were taken over by the German authorities. The boys were told to collect all their belongings and go home. They would be notified through the columns of the *Evening Post* when classes would resume at the new location of Halkett Place Girls' School. The girls were accommodated at Le Coie Hall in Janvrin Road, St Helier.

Another highly successful production by Kenneth Britton and Richard Whinnerah,
for which the author was the choreographer, was 'No, No, Nanette'
with Betty Le Heeray and Ken Guiton in the leading roles.

It was hard for me to take in that the old cricket field where I had once received half a crown from the Head for both scoring 50 not out and taking a hat-trick in the same match was being used as a training ground for German troops. The thought of such things made me so angry that I wished desperately that I could be away and fighting them instead of having to obey their wretched orders.

A soap ration of one tablet per person was decreed. Like many other things, it was only for one week.

The opening play of the winter season 1941/2 was a particularly successful production of *Yellow Sands* by Eden Phillpots, produced by Max Le Feuvre for the Green Room Club. It had been done two years before at the Opera House by an English repertory company headed by Graham Pocket. The Annual General Meeting of the Green Room Club was presided over by the Acting President, Max Le Feuvre, as the President, Major-General Willis, had left the Island. It was clear that there was a strong demand from the public for productions to continue, and the election of officers brought few changes. I was once more elected to the Committee.

The Club immediately persuaded me to put on a revue entitled *What's Next?* in November 1941. I decided to use a large cast so as to give a chance to as many people as possible to perform. There was to be a good mixture of song, dance and sketches and, of course, I took care of the dancing. Arthur Guiton directed the singing, and the orchestra was under the direction of Roy McKee.

The show was produced under duress. Material for costumes was difficult to find and lighting was also a problem. The reduced hours of gas supply interfered with rehearsals and with dressmaking, but Madame Blondeau who made costumes for us as always did an excellent job. We were given a warm reception. The profits from this show went to local charities.

One of the delights of this production for me was to have my wife, dancing under her maiden name of Irene Newland, as my partner once again. I said earlier that we had married only shortly before the Occupation. For some time before that we had gone round with a jolly group of young people, and Irene and I had found that we both had the same interests.

More than anything, we loved dancing together. She was a natural dancer with great talent, inherited no doubt from her family as two of her aunts were well-known dancers in both London and New York. One, Carrie Graham, was the choreographer for the André Charlot revues.

The Green Room Club finished the year by producing *Tilly of Bloomsbury* by Ian Hay on December 29th, presented once more by Kenneth Britton and Richard Winnerah. It was a very bright play and a good one for the holiday.

Still the orders flowed. All subjects of the USA over the age of 15 were required to report to the German authorities, now stationed at College House. Those under 15 had to be registered orally or in writing by their guardian. Such persons were not allowed to leave the place where they were staying. This was also to apply to Jews, who found themselves in trouble for the slightest offence.

People with cattle in their custody were required to specify the number and the authorities were to assess the amount of milk that should be produced from them. We felt that they would be watching farmers milk the cows pretty soon.

During December 1941 the authorities made an effort to give us some extras for Christmas and the New Year: a ration of 2oz of tea, 1oz of cocoa, for everyone, and (something new) 2oz of chocolate (three bars) for those under 18. Oranges were available on the junior ration book, but on the German ration books as well! There was also a ration of 2oz of pipe tobacco. Good news was that the electricity supply was extended until midnight.

We had quite a good Christmas. My aunt came along with her dog for the day. The District Nurse, who still had a ration of petrol as she had quite a large area to cover, brought her up in her car, which I suppose, strictly speaking, she should not have done.

Mrs Newland had saved up to make a Christmas pudding and I had managed to obtain a duck from a good farmer friend who also promised to keep for me a pair of young ones in the spring. These would be safer to keep than chickens as they could make quite a noise if anyone tried to steal them. My aunt made some mince pies and, with a bottle of wine, we drank this toast: 'To the end of the Occupation, all absent friends and all our other hopes for the years ahead.'

We made use of the extra hours of electricity on those days and played cards by way of a change but, as the year changed, Irene and I were even more aware that we were wasting our lives. Our thoughts were with our friends who were far away and we wondered about them all.

One very sad piece of news was the death of the former Bailiff, Mr Charles Edward Malet de Carteret, aged 72. This was quite a loss to the Island's administration. He had been educated at Victoria College and had passed into Sandhurst in 1886, coming first on the list of Cavalry Cadets. He was then gazetted to the Royal Enniskillen Dragoons, later returning to the Island.

As the winter passed, we started to think about what we should be planting in the garden, now that the entire lawn had been dug up. I spent a good deal of time visiting the nearby farms trying to buy seed potatoes. It was all very difficult as many farmers had not retained the amount of seed that they should have done and there had been a great demand. At the same time, I tried to obtain extra milk as we were worried about Mr Newland's health as he had lost quite a lot of weight. We felt it might be beneficial to add a little more milk to his diet. Eventually I was able to obtain seed potatoes and the promise of two pints of milk per week at two separate farms, which was indeed fortunate. Kindling wood became our next concern. Both Irene and I were to spend a considerable time on this job, which we called 'wooding'.

Meanwhile, the theatre school was growing. Many of the girls who belonged to the Green Room Club had joined, hoping to be in more productions. Miss Mary Burger had joined the staff and was in charge of Elocution. I was obliged to spend more time at the studio and, as Faldouet where we lived was about four miles from St Helier, that meant a lot of cycling in cold weather. How we missed our car! Mrs Newland went into town by bus, which was always packed, but her husband hardly ever stirred from the house. He was just not well enough and was quite happy to stroll around the garden when the weather was good enough.

By now all the orders in the *Evening Post* were signed by Feld Kommandant Knackfuss. Up to now changes had been followed by strict orders and enforcement, but people appeared to ignore most of them although a few individuals were caught.

My father had again received news of my brother who was now in South Africa. I saw very little of my father who had married again, but I did call on him from time to time to see how he was faring.

We were allowed half a pint of cooking oil per person for one week, for which one had to provide the bottles. This was very welcome as we had had none so far. Washing powder and one tablet of soap, 1lb of jam and 4oz of chocolate were also available. It is hard to imagine how welcome these small amounts were. The very thought of the soap made me feel cleaner.

We feared that this would be followed by something not so good and so it proved. The hours of gas were again reduced from March 14th and would be supplied from 7am to 2pm and from 5pm to 9pm.

All people with harbour permits now had to present them with one passport-sized photograph to the authorities before March 15th, and those holding a fishing permit had to do the same, with two photographs. By this stage I had lost count of how many times these permits had been changed.

The Green Room Club was eager to put on *The Pirates of Penzance* and an advertisement was placed in the *Evening Post* for musical scores and libretti to be sent to the Honorary Secretary, Mrs Helen Sinnett. Fortunately, enough were found to enable the Club to put on a very good production, produced by Max Le Feuvre and under the musical direction of Lyndon Marguerie LRAM. In spite of problems in finding the costumes, the Pirates really looked the part. It was good to have a Gilbert and Sullivan show as a change of genre was needed.

Although there was already a large number of German troops on the Island, we were now besieged by 'Hitler's Youth', who were arriving in droves. Some estimates put the figure at 10,000, with more to follow. Hotels were commandeered to house them, and Victoria College had also been taken over. Sad to say, the College sports ground was turned into a builder's yard. It seemed that there were now more troops on the Island than civilians.

Another most stupid order dealt with articles that must not be purchased by the German forces. None of these items were available in any case, stocks having been finished long before the notice appeared. The Germans had the habit of issuing orders and then changing, cancelling or repeating them several weeks later. The end-result was utter confusion.

In 1942 the Germans celebrated Hitler's birthday (April 20th) in a big way. They decorated all their cars, carts and lorries with flowers. All did not go smoothly, however. During the evening an officer who was making a speech about his beloved Fuehrer was shot by one of his men, who then committed suicide. 'Pity that it wasn't Hitler himself,' I thought.

An aggressive act from the enemy made me think that the Islanders should make an official appeal. An elderly local resident was sentenced to twelve months' imprisonment for defending his wife when a German officer snatched at an RAF broach she was wearing. Surely the officer was the one to be punished.

The Germans took over Huelin's building store at Five Oaks and turned it into an ammunition dump. We heard that they had had a big shooting match up there among themselves, which must have alarmed nearby residents. It can't have been a pleasant neighbourhood in which to live during those unhappy times.

TROOPS ON PARADE: General Freiherr von Richtofen, under whose proclamation the island was occupied by the German Air Force, reviewing officers and men at St Brelade's.
(Photo courtesy Jersey Evening Post)

There were also several instances of what I called 'carelessness' on the part of the soldiers. A landmine exploded killing one of them at Portelet, followed by two more at the airport and several others in various parts of the Island. We were also told that a number of officers had committed suicide.

CHAPTER THREE

ON WITH THE SHOW

Meanwhile I had been far from idle, aside from my daily home chores. A production for the theatre school was under consideration, and some of the pupils were wondering just how soon they would have the opportunity to perform. It was clear that they loved working with me and my dance arrangements, and we were very eager to display the abilities of the school.

Irene and I discussed it at length. As we wanted everybody to be in it in some way or other, it had to be in the form of a Revue, and it could not be entirely dancing as we did not as yet have anything like that amount of talent. The people available would have to be split up into various groups, according to their particular abilities, with special items for the children. The Elocution Department was not strong enough to handle the sketches, so I would have to invite some members of the Green Room Club to help out with that as well as with the singing. I think that this was the most difficult production that I have ever dealt with.

I realised that costumes would not be easy to make, but worst of all would be finding suitable sketches and music because the supply was limited to what was already on the Island. However, I was determined to do my best for them all as that was, after all, my intention when I started the school. I was completely dedicated to keeping up the morale of as many people as possible: not only the children but also their parents, families and friends.

Once I had announced my plans everyone became very excited. This was to be their first school production and would be entitled *Happy Faces*. I asked the students to collect any material that could be used for making costumes. I would then have to design a wide variety for all the musical numbers we were wanting to present. At the beginning the only item I had decided on was 'Me and My Girl' for the children, with little Sally Noel and John Hibbs (aged five) as the principals. They were great. John was in later years to become the popular Headmaster of Victoria College Preparatory School.

The Opera House opened its doors to *Happy Faces* on April 27th 1942. To judge by the applause it went quite well. The *Evening Post* was kind enough to

The cast of 'Happy Days' on the stage at the Opera House, Jersey.

say that it should appeal to the public as they would find much to amuse them in it. I was so glad to have broken the ice without falling through. The students were so eager for success that it helped to carry the day and they did not fail me. I was grateful to the valuable help given by the Green Room Club guest artists and to Madame Blondeau who was so very clever with the costumes.

Charcoal for running the buses was now being produced locally in sufficient quantities to restore services. After tests, it was believed that it should be possible to continue to run the buses on charcoal as long as there was a supply of wood. This was indeed good news, and parents were glad that children living in rural areas could get to schools in St Helier.

In addition to the German marks in

AT THE STAGE DOOR. Above: Sally Noel and John Hibbs. Below: Some of the 'Happy Days' cast.

circulation, a currency of local notes designed by the well-known Jersey artist Edmund Blampied was introduced. The notes were most attractive and many were being acquired as souvenirs. I myself was able to procure a set.

Our gardener came for only four hours a week and so there was plenty to do. Potatoes, vegetables, sugarbeet and tobacco were the main items we grew, but in addition there were gooseberries, black and red currants, raspberries and fruit trees.

There was a gate at the end of our garden where the vegetables were grown, out of sight of the house. One or two of the German troops who were stationed at the end of the road had discovered that they could make their way through the garden, passing in front of the house, to get to Gorey Hill, thus cutting off quite a distance. But they really had their eye on the fruit and were just waiting their chance. The locals who knew the place would also most likely take a chance.

My dog, Timmy, hated the Germans. I think that the smell of the uniforms enraged him, and he would bark at them all the way across the garden. We were always afraid that they would shoot him. Some of them were very cheeky and if anyone was in the sun lounge, they would walk slowly by and stare.

In the Parish of St Martin's a cow was stolen. Anything could vanish overnight, but it had most likely been taken during the day from the field where it was tethered in a high, wired enclosure with a locked gate. Whoever stole it killed it right away and most likely sold the meat on the black market. A reward was offered, without results. Eventually, the remains of the animal were traced. The entrails and udder were buried in sacks at a depth of four feet in one place, the horns under a tree and the jaw bone in a small chicken run. An arrest was made later on, but who the culprit was remained a mystery.

Immediately after this the Germans issued an order that all cattle out to pasture had to be stabled or brought near to the farm building. I could not see that that would in any way prevent someone stealing a cow if they had set their mind to it.

I was amazed at the frequency and variety of orders concerning identification which appeared. The latest one was the requirement for the names in full, date and place of birth and nationality of each civilian residing in each house to be registered. If anyone should stay over three days or if any child were born it was the duty of the householder immediately to inform the Chief Registration Officer. The name of the house, the street and the parish and all details had to be supplied in triplicate. One copy was to be kept in the house as it was the duty of the police to visit every place of residence to ascertain that the declaration was correct.

I did feel that half the orders were meant to annoy us, or perhaps to catch

Currency notes
designed by
Jersey artist
Edmund Blampied

*Above and right: Front and back of
10 shilling note.*

*Below: Front and back of
2 shilling note.*

*Above and right: Front and back of
1 shilling note*

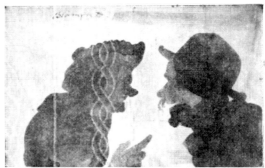

Below: Front and back of 6 pence note

someone out so that the Germans could collect a fine or imprison them. I thought they were a dastardly lot and expected that we should soon have to give toe and fingerprints.

The next thing was that we had to register our bicycles, unlicensed or licensed, and anyone failing to comply rendered himself or herself liable to severe penalties. Irene and I both had to obey this order as our bicycles were an absolute necessity.

The public were again reminded that, in accordance with the German military law and in agreement with the Hague Convention, the penalty for espionage and sabotage was death. It seemed that the authorities were becoming apprehensive. They warned that when the sirens were sounded, people must clear the streets and seek shelter. We wondered if they really thought that the British would bomb the Island. Could it be that the Germans' planes would bomb us by mistake? We believed that Britain certainly would never bomb the Channel Islands.

Because of the rife unemployment in the 1930s many nationals of the Irish Free State had come to Jersey to work on the farms during the potato season. On the whole they were an unruly lot, causing a great deal of trouble. Many were stranded at the beginning of the Occupation, but they had hoped to escape from having to comply with the orders and restrictions imposed on the Islanders. Some were even openly sympathetic to the Germans. However, in the spring of 1942 they were required to report to the German Authorities with their passports – for them an unexpected shock.

In May 1942 yet another German notice regarding wireless sets was published. People with more than one set were required to take them to the German Authorities as the Army of Occupation was in need of these and radiograms. On a previous occasion people had had to hand in sets because of the painting of 'V' signs.

The Germans also issued a notice to the effect that the confiscation of wirelesses should not be regarded as a punishment but as a measure taken for military reasons. To ensure an orderly collection the date of delivery was extended to June 20th.

Following this the *British Pamphlet No 1 of the British Patriots* was published. It urged us not to give up our wirelesses and to repute the German assertion that the confiscation was covered by the Hague Convention. Rumours flew around that many people were being interrogated and arrested over this.

A pound of biscuits was given free on the children's ration books up to the age of 18, and on the German ration book. The biscuits were a gift, thanks to the co-operation of local grocers, from the French Secours National. We felt we could do with a few more gifts.

One of Noel Coward's greatest successes, *Hay Fever*, was produced by Mrs Dorothy Stevenson, an ex-professional actress. She created a theatre out of a school hall, built a stage and did an outstanding job. I was fortunate to be cast as Sandy, a lovely part which suited me down to the ground. The play was a tremendous success, one of the best produced on the Island during this period. The entire profits were donated to Grouville Parish Charities.

One of the strangest orders ever to be given to the farmers by the Feld Kommandant was to the effect that the harvest must 'begin at once'. I thought that the farmers themselves would have been the best judges of when harvesting should be done, and in any case harvesting had already begun some time before the order. A short time before this, an entire load of stooks and a horse-drawn van were stolen from a large field in broad daylight. Strange to say we heard nothing more about it.

During the threshing season the Germans sent inspectors round the farms. Many of them had themselves been farmers before the war, and they were quite willing to help on the farms, as long as they were well fed. They turned a blind eye to anything untoward that might be taking place.

Douglas Le Marquand was killed while trying to escape with four of his friends. The time of burial was kept quiet, as was news of the entire episode, because the Germans were afraid it might incite demonstrations.

A German plane crashed at Corbiere. These accidents were a common occurrence, but the Germans were adept at concealing the news. I expected that they would claim that this particular plane was British.

There were several reported cases of people suspected of collaborating with our oppressors. Some houses had even been adorned with swastikas, possibly by locals. There is little doubt that some deserved the emblem. It was too bad that some Island girls could not resist the attention of the soldiers: we called them 'Gerry bags'. They would very likely suffer for this after the war was over.

The Germans have ordered that no cereals should be sown, but that vegetables should be planted instead. This meant that they would probably commandeer the cereal seed – some six hundred tonnes.

I received a notice from the 'Department of Transport', issued by the Feld Kommandant, that two employees would call on me in a few days' time to make an evaluation on my car etc etc. They duly arrived and I had my story ready.

I informed them that a considerable time before, on a date I could not remember, four officers had turned up in a car and demanded to see it. I told them that I did not want to sell. When they had looked at it, they told me that they were ordered to collect any car that they saw fit. I had demanded to see an order to this effect, but I was told that I could not question the orders of Der Militarbefahrshaben and I was to hand over the keys at once. I had delayed for some time, but they became angry and threatened me, so I had handed over the keys. They had driven off and that was the last that I saw of the car, but I had an idea that soon after that, when I was in town, I had caught sight of it in the distance. I hoped that this story would be accepted.

I was then asked why I had not reported it missing. My reply was that I would have had to turn it in at some time anyway, so it would not have made much difference. I had seen no point in going through endless complications. They appeared to accept this and departed to make their report. The possibility of my car being discovered in its hiding place at some future date would certainly land me in trouble. I would have to make up another story, but I was still determined that they would not have my car.

On the night of May 3rd/4th, three youths equipped with binoculars and compass attempted to reach England in a motorboat. Tragically the boat capsized. One young man was drowned and the other two were captured. We did not know what the punishment was, but the Island was warned that if there was a repetition of such an attempt the whole population would suffer. Such news brought home to us the isolation and danger of our position.

The *Evening Post* was obliged to close down as it had run out of paper. Fortunately this situation did not last for long, however.

Despite the reported mining of the coastal region, the Department of Agriculture received notification from the German Field Command that a certain number of slipways leading to the beaches would be open for the purpose of gathering vraic, the seaweed used as a fertiliser on the fields. This was rather an eye-opener. Or was it a trap to catch the British if the news were to be passed on? The farmers were, of course, delighted as vraic had been used quite extensively in normal times and at low water one would see vraic carts going down to cut it off the rocks.

Happy-go-Lucky, the school's second revue, was an instant success when it opened at the Opera House for one week on September 14th 1942. The school had grown tremendously and I was fortunate in having dance students who were also good singers.

All in all it turned out to be a very exciting production. Many people had wondered how I would manage such a large company but, with careful grouping, a good result and a beautiful finale were achieved. It was the first time I had choreographed a ballet for Irene and myself, which we called 'Knave among the Hearts'. The King, mostly a mime part, was played by Bert Hibbs who could always look stately in costume. Irene was the Queen of Hearts, I played the Knave and the corps de ballet were the one to ten of Hearts. It was well received.

The finale of the first part of the show was devoted to sea songs and shanties.

The dancers were divided into five groups to give everyone a chance to perform. The costumes were simple but effective, with the girls in white shorts wearing matelot caps and the men in white slacks, blue shirts and caps kindly lent by the Yacht Club.

A grand scene including the numbers 'Join the Navy' and 'Crest of a Wave' caused a small riot. The applause was tremendous and some of the audience were so excited that they stood on the seats, clapping and singing 'Join the Navy'. We were amazed and delighted by the effect of this, and I was glad for all those who took part both on and off stage that we had achieved what we hoped to do, to give pleasure to so many people.

I thought a little talk was

Knave among the Hearts

needed on stage before the second night. I asked the cast to act like 'pros' and not to get carried away by the success of the first night. The excitement was still with us, however, and I received plenty of compliments, many from people I did not know.

In spite of the demonstration I hoped that I would be able to continue, although I expected to be summoned to give an explanation about the riot.

Sure enough, on October 12th I received the following translation by the Bailiff of a notification from the Feld Kommandant, Dr Casper: 'Demonstration during an Entertainment. It has come to my attention that a performance at a Theatre in which uniforms resembling those of the British Navy were shown degenerated into a demonstration. I request, therefore, that you will take steps to see that no uniforms which could be confused with military uniforms will be shown.' As the show had been over for three weeks, I immediately sent my written compliance with this request.

```
Field Command 515,
AM. Pol. 02 - II                          12th. October 1942.

                    TRANSLATION

The Bailiff of Jersey.
          Demonstration during an Entertainment.

It has come to my attention that a performance at a Theatre
in which uniforms resembling those of the British Navy were
shown, degenerated into a demonstration.

I request, therefore, that you will take steps to see that
no uniforms which could be confused with military uniforms
will be shown.

                    For the Field Commandant,
                    Dr. Casper. O.K.V.R.
```

The beginning of the next term presented a problem as I now had many more applications to join the school, all with the idea of getting on the stage. With over a hundred students already, I did not know whether I should be able to cope with more and I had to explain that, owing to the size of the school, I would now have to limit the numbers who were to perform and I would have to hold auditions.

The following are items of news in brief:

1. Traffic control men have been told to salute German officers. Often their rather dilatory effort is anything but polite.

2. Another, more ridiculous order was that islanders were forbidden to leave for the Continent – as if we could!

3. The Germans ransacked the Masonic Temple, which quite upset my father, who was a Mason. They were also enquiring about church plate.

4. A German plane transporting troops crashed into the sea at St Catherine's. Apparently there were no survivors.

5. Two land mines exploded, one at La Colette where many windows were shattered, and one at Bel Royal.

6. Many troops are being taken off the Island, together with stores and equipment. The grapevine has it that they are being sent to Africa. Most of them do not seem to be happy about this move.

7. The States have decided to take possession of any neglected gardens and plots of land. They would put this to good use, as well as providing work for the unemployed.

8. Jersey people were saddened to learn of the sinking of both the destroyer HMS *Jersey* and the Great Western Railway mailboat *St Patrick*.

On September 16th and 21st we were delighted to receive two Red Cross messages, one from an aunt in Southampton saying that my brother, on leave in South Africa, was well, and the other direct from him in Sierra Leone: 'Anxious for news, none from you or relatives in Vancouver.'

British subjects were being deported to Germany at this time. Their departure date had been delayed before and once more they were having to stand by because of weather. It was a horrible situation for them, wondering what they were going to. Irene's parents would have been among them if Mr Newland had not been so ill. He had now lost two stone in weight.

The Green Room Club continued to be very busy: *Trial by Jury* was the next production. It was so good to see Gilbert and Sullivan again. This was followed the next month by Sir James Barrie's *Dear Brutus*, produced by Mr H.B.Coley. It was an excellent play and much appreciated.

We were again amused by the reams of 'Exchange and Mart': Exchange young goat for lady's cycle; Football boots size 8 for size 2; Pram with canopy for cycle; Canary and seed for pram wheels; Barrel of cider for equal value of gin or whisky; Sow due to farrow for mangolds [cattle feed], hay or straw; White blanket for coloured blanket; Baby doll and pram for gramophone records.'

Also amusing was this item: 'A young lady working in Guernsey has become engaged through a twenty-five word "proposal" from a male friend through the Red Cross. The answer was, simply, "Yes".'

More items of food were available on ration: dates, coffee substitute, canned peas, cheese and 4ozs of boiled sweets.

If a horse was offered for sale, the Feld Kommandant had first option on it for one week. Should anyone buy it before the seven days were out, he was liable to prison and a fine.

I felt by now that the Germans were perceptibly on the defensive. Obviously the war news was not coming up to their expectations and they were now displaying a little more muscle.

No lights must appear from any building. A blue light was permitted for exits which led from passageways and screened lighting must be used when absolutely necessary for the maintenance of traffic. This, of course, was nothing new to us but it appeared to be a sign of nervous tension on their part. Of late troops had been marching along our road at night which, of course, made me aware of the curfew. I must be sure to be home in time.

The German food office was asking for people to supply cats and dogs that were good ratters and mousers. I wondered if they were a little hungry for meat? I know that later on they were offering a bottle of brandy for a fat cat or dog. They actually caught my aunt's spaniel which was seen with a German soldier about two miles from home. Fortunately, it must have escaped as it arrived home safely.

The Green Room Club lived up to its reputation and produced its annual pantomime, shortly followed by *Interference* by Robert Pertwee, produced by Dennis Ryan. This was quite a change of pace as it was a stirring drama. I could remember being in another production of the same play with the Denville Players years before.

It seemed strange to me that I was never called to account for the 'demonstration' in the last production. When the time came for the next show to be prepared, I had to submit the script for inspection and I was called to College House to explain the meaning of some of the words in it. One of the lines in the opening chorus was 'Look up to the sky', which referred to the sunshine. They thought it meant looking for the RAF and the line had to be altered. There were other similar lines which were deleted. They did not seem to believe my explanations.

One funny little advertisement which I cut out of the newspaper was this: 'For sale: "Mother's Ruin" by Ivah Few, "Don't be vague" by A.Little.' I wonder who had a good supply of gin – and would it be at black market prices?

Our Christmas 1942 was more or less a duplicate of the one before. It was very quiet. The news from England appeared to be a little brighter.

Our third revue, *Happy Returns*, opened on March 6th 1943. I continued to use the word 'Happy' in the title and intended always to do so. We played to full houses all the week, although it

Orchid and Cactus

was not possible to repeat the rapturous acclaim of the previous revue. Our script was now under close scrutiny and it was, in any case, difficult to find suitable material.

About a week after the production I was again called on to attend College House. I was somewhat apprehensive but I could think of nothing that might have got me into trouble. The script had been passed by the authorities and had not been altered. The usual box at the rear of the Dress Circle at the Opera House had been, as always, reserved for officials to vet the production. As our shows were always fully booked there were no other seats available for the soldiers but, in any case, this was all in the hands of the management of the theatre.

I was ushered into the room which I remembered as our Headmaster's study, although when I had previously submitted scripts it had been in the Dining Room. A Kommandant whom I had not met before rose from his desk, greeted me and shook hands, a new departure. He was smiling and most affable. He was already drinking brandy and offered me one. Although I felt a little embarrassed, I decided that I had better accept.

When I was comfortably seated with a drink in hand, he informed me that he had attended *Happy Returns* and was full of admiration and congratulations. He thought the entire show first class. The 'Blue Danube' number was unquestionably superb, he said. Quickly I took a gulp of the brandy. I was astounded and knocked speechless by what followed: 'I would like you to bring the entire production to Germany and I will fly you all there.'

It took me some time to gather my thoughts. I would like to have said, 'You must be kidding!' I think that he was amused at my expression. I took another gulp and thanked him for the honour that he was bestowing on our production but, I said, it would be impossible to accept his invitation as I had many young people in the cast and their parents would never agree to their leaving the Island. It would be far too dangerous at this time...perhaps after the war was over?

After a few more fruitless attempts at persuasion, seeing that I was adamant he gave up and changed the subject. He said that he found Jersey a beautiful Island and hoped to come back again some day but, for the time being, he had a job to do. He spoke more about the beauty of the Island, the bays and the countryside and never referred to the subject of the war. He was certainly not a Nazi. While he was on the Island he intended to see all my productions. I thanked him, shook hands again and departed. It had been a strange meeting indeed.

As I walked away I wondered about him. How very different he was from the other man I had met over the script. He was so polite and so full of understanding. Had he not been my enemy, I would have enjoyed his acquaintance. At the same time I prayed that he would not appear backstage at any future shows of mine, in case it was thought that I was consorting with the enemy.

At about this time there was a further development in the provision of wooden soled shoes. Sabot boots were to be imported from France. At the same time wooden soled shoes, known as 'the Jersey Shoe', were to be manufactured by the States' Textiles Department. They were well constructed with an oil-dressed upper, a wooden sole with strips of rubber, and metal toe and heel. The soles had to be repaired from time to time. These were initially available for women agricultural workers and were later made for children also. Certainly many people were in desperate need of clothes and footwear.

Miss Joan Picot in 'Les Cloches de Corneville'

Over the weeks various items were available on ration for one week: tunny fish, one tin for 1s; 8oz macaroni; 1lb pot of jam; one tablet of soap; one bottle of wine; coffee substitute; 8oz salt at one penny for 3oz. Members of the public who required potatoes had to register with the name and address of a retailer. Everything we required involved paperwork.

A consignment of working trousers was available for men and youths in certain sizes. Application had to be made for a permit to buy them. They were in great demand as it was a very long time since we had been able to purchase such items.

A heifer was stolen from a cowshed. I imagine that it was soon devoured. It would certainly never be found as many people were now hungry. The rations did not satisfy appetites at all.

The Green Room Club presented *Les Cloches de Corneville*, a charming musical. One of my students, Miss Joan Picot, who was a lovely singer, took the lead. Mr Max Le Feuvre was the producer and Mr Lyndon Marguerie the conductor. By this time the evening performance began at 6.30pm so that people could return home before curfew.

The Military were responsible for a shocking accident at St John's. In many parts of the Island railway tracks had been put down over good farmland with complete disregard for the rights of the owners of the property. A farmer had gone out to see to his cattle and when he did not return, his son went out to look for him. He was horrified to find the mutilated body of his father near the railway line and his left arm some 25 yards away. The father was said to be stone deaf. This was a tragedy for the family but we never heard what reaction there was from the Military Authorities.

Soon after this came the news that the bodies of two non-commissioned officers of the RAF, Sergeants D.C.Butten and A.Halden, had been washed ashore on the coast of the Island. A service was held in the hospital chapel. It was led by the Dean of Jersey, assisted by the Chairman of the Methodist Church, and attended by the Bailiff and Members of the States of Jersey, the Red Cross, the British Legion and the Royal Air Force Association. Also present was a German officer, representing the German Military Authorities.

At the conclusion of the service the coffins, which had rested in the chapel, were covered with a Union Jack and carried to the waiting hearses. On each coffin was placed a wreath from the States of Jersey and one from the German Air Force. The hearses proceeded to the cemetery at Mont à l'Abbé, followed by coaches carrying official representatives.

The ceremony was then taken over by the German Air Force. Each coffin was carried by six men of the German Air Force. After the final rites had been performed by the Dean of Jersey, the Guard of Honour presented arms. This was immediately followed by the traditional military salute of three rounds of fire. Although the general public was officially forbidden from attending the ceremonies, nevertheless many people visited the graves during the day and over a hundred floral tributes were placed on them.In this situation the military certainly made an attempt to impress the public, but this was not always so unfortunately. They shot down two paratroopers who had baled out over the sea from a plane that was limping home. This was hardly an act to gain favour with the local population.

The following drastic and unwelcome notice appeared in the *Evening Post*:

'Proceedings will not be taken against any person who surrenders his wireless receiving set by December 31 1942. Otherwise, he will be imprisoned with hard labour and, in some cases, will be punished with the death penalty.'

We duly handed in three sets, keeping one back. Life without any news would have been intolerable.

One of my expeditions in search of eggs or anything in the way of foodstuffs led me to visit the Bernards' farm. As I rounded the bend of the avenue on my bicycle and turned into the farmyard, there was a uniformed soldier standing beside a motor cycle with sidecar. Since he was obviously staring at me, I decided that there should be no turning back.

The three Bernard children were playing around a wheelbarrow filled with swedes, and when they saw me they came running to greet me. Mary, the eldest (age seven), informed me that her father and mother were with two German officers who had been searching the house for a long time. She appeared quite anxious.

The two younger children, on the other hand, seemed unconcerned by this grave situation. They clammered for a ride on my bicycle. I at once put one on the saddle, the other on the crossbar and wheeled them to the barrow near the shed where they had been playing. Ann, the little one, spotted a ball resting on the top of the swedes and immediately climbed to retrieve it.

Meanwhile the soldier continued to stare. I had the feeling that I was not wanted but I took no notice. When Ann threw the ball towards him, he simply ambled away towards the house and leaned against the doorway, obviously not interested in children. After we had all played with the ball for a little while, Ann climbed back onto the barrow.

When Mrs Louise Bernard emerged from the house she was so glad to see me that she at once came over to explain that the Germans had been in the house for over two hours searching for a wireless. She was most annoyed as they were turning everything upside down, even opening her jewelry case, and in desperation she had finally left them with her husband.

We walked round to the garden in front of the house to pick some flowers, followed at a distance by the soldier who was determined to watch us. However, he seemed rather disappointed when Mary ran back to keep her eye on the little ones. When we came back into the yard we put the flowers in my cycle basket as though that had been part of my mission. At the same time, the officers at last came out of the house followed by Mr Bernard. They spoke to the soldiers for a minute or two, staring at me most of the time, I expect wondering why I was there.

Finally one came over to the children and asked them where the wireless was. Mr Bernard was furious and told them to leave the children alone. The Germans had already been told that the Bernards did not have one, and in any case they had just searched the house. But he again repeated the question to John, the four- year-old. He nodded his head and said, 'Wire, wire,' then started to cross the yard. The officer then turned his head with a broad smile of victory and slowly followed the child across into the shed.

Meanwhile Ann and Mary sat on the barrow, watched intently by the other officers and soldiers. Mr and Mrs Bernard showed no expression and waited. A few minutes later the officer stormed out shouting to the others and flinging a small roll of wire across to us, followed by little John in floods of tears. They climbed into the sidecar and roared out of the yard. We all laughed as Mr Bernard rushed forward and picked up John, telling him that he was a very clever little boy, and one day he would be a great man.

We left the children playing in the yard and went into the house to have a glass of cider. I came away with a small bottle of milk, half a dozen eggs and a bottle of cider. It had been quite a morning, with John quite unconsciously the star of the show. It was lovely to have seen those kind people again, and to know that they were doing their best to outwit the enemy and at the same time doing their best to help others. 'By the way,' said Mr Bernard, 'if you would like to know, the wireless is in a tin box in the barrow of swedes. Of course we will have to find another place in case they come snooping around again.'

It was a wonderful ending as we could all have a good laugh at our enemy in spite of our trials and tribulations.

CHAPTER FOUR

SKIRMISH WITH THE GESTAPO

On Wednesday March 3rd 1943, after an anonymous letter was sent to the Gestapo, a Mr Tierney was arrested. The following day Jack Nicolle and his father were both arrested. Ruby Nicolle, Jack's wife, who was our maid, came to work the next morning in a miserable state. Her husband was very ill with yellow jaundice and she had hoped to be able to take food to the prison for him, but had not been allowed to.

The following Thursday, when she was due to come to us, she rang to say that she had been ordered by the Gestapo to go to their headquarters at Silvertide, Havre des Pas, and so would be late for work. She did not turn up that day, nor the next and on the Saturday afternoon her stepfather rang to say that she had been taken directly from Silvertide to prison.

After that, news filtered through that various people had been taken in for questioning. This was all very disturbing.

On the evening of March 18th the phone rang and, jokingly, I said, 'It must be the Secret Police!' It turned out to be a very poor joke indeed because it was in fact the Gestapo with the request that Mrs Newland should be at Silvertide the following morning. At that time we did not know why Ruby or the others had been arrested but we felt that it must be connected with the radio which we knew her husband had. She had been bringing the news to us but we decided there and then that we had no knowledge of any wireless or news of any kind and would certainly not give her away if that was what we were to be questioned about. She, of course, had no knowledge of our wireless as we had never told anyone.

Mrs Newland caught the bus first thing in the morning and hoped to return home by midday. There were only a few buses each day. At 12.30pm the phone rang and we at once thought that she had missed the bus. But no, it was the Secret Police asking me to be at Silvertide, with my wife, at 2.30pm. I asked to speak to Mrs Newland but they did not answer. We did not know what to think.

In a frantic rush we had lunch and decided that Mr Newland should go to bed in case they sent for him. We put on a change of clothing and Irene packed her and her mother's jewelry and all the money we had in the house. If it got around that we were all away and the house empty it would soon have been ransacked.

We went on our bicycles and on the way we called at our friends, the Allports, quickly explained matters to them and left our valuables. They agreed that, if we did not return, they would arrange for someone to take care of Mr Newland, who was now in bed, and to feed Timmy the dog.

We parked our cycles at the studio and walked the rest of the way to Silvertide. Our minds were by now in complete turmoil.

At Silvertide a man in uniform wearing dark glasses showed us into a room on the ground floor and we were told not to speak. It was obvious that things were very serious. Mrs Newland was seated in another part of the room and Irene and I were at once separated. I wondered if Mrs Newland had had any lunch. She looked very tired.

In what follows, I can only recount at first hand my own part, as I heard the experiences of the other two after the affair was over.

When Irene and I were finally seated, it was arranged so that we could hardly see each other. Another man was seated at a desk and was busy writing. He kept this up for some time, no doubt to make us nervous. At last he came over, took my identification papers and proceeded to ask me routine questions about my place of birth, address, whether I had any children etc, but also whether I had ever been punished for any misdeeds. After a few words with the first man, he took me to a room upstairs. As I passed Mrs Newland I could see that she was looking pretty grim. I felt that she would have liked to say something but dared not.

He placed me at a table facing a dazzling light, and I could feel heat behind me. He seated himself by a window and then proceeded to tell me that I must speak the truth. He asked me if I knew Mrs Nicolle. I said that I did and that she was my mother-in-law's maid. Then he asked me, 'What about the news she brings every day, written on a piece of paper in pencil?' I denied any knowledge of this and said that we had never received any news at any time from anyone, whereupon his tone of voice changed and he became more severe. He said that within an hour I would know what a mistake I had made. Mrs Newland had made the same mistake and it was evident that we had decided to tell the same story. Maybe my wife would not be so stupid.

It was, of course, quite true. We had all agreed to make the same reply. He was used to being the inquisitor and continued in a harsher vein, repeating the same questions and adding, with much venom, 'You will see! You will see!' I must say that with both the heat and the strong light I was feeling far from comfortable, but I did not think that I had shown any disquiet over his questioning. I was determined to try to hold my own, so I asked him in as quiet a voice as I could muster, what he meant by saying I had made a mistake. Once again he said, 'You will see!'

He then turned his back on me and stood gazing out of the window as though time were of no consequence, before repeating the words, 'You will see!' It was all part of the act, a performance to try to frighten me. After more delay, he said that if I did not tell him the truth I would be sent to prison and court-martialled and that within four days I would be sent to a concentration camp for two years.

I tried to play his game and so I paused before again saying that I was telling the truth. He screamed, 'Lies! Lies!' Calmly I replied that I could say that we had received news from Mrs Nicolle but that it was not true. He kept repeating the same things in a manner that seemed really neurotic. I said, 'I am sorry that you doubt my veracity.' This provoked another loud scream. I think my calmness annoyed him. I was not so calm inside, however, and by that time I had a severe headache. I asked for a drink. No reply. He calmed down a little and said that my lovely wife would suffer the same penalty.

I was then told to follow him downstairs. As I passed Mrs Newland, I watched her and I thought that she was trying to say, 'Ruby confessed.' I could not be certain as she made no sound and I was not close enough to be sure, but it gave me food for thought. I decided that I would not change my story.

Poor Irene was taken upstairs for her turn. I felt so much for her in that hot room and under the glare of the light, and going through the same routine, with him trying to play us off against the other, but I knew that she would be strong and that he would not get the result he wanted. She would most likely tell him not to shout at her.

I was unable to see Mrs Newland from where I was sitting, but I knew just how worried she would be about her husband. At such a time, a thousand thoughts fly through one's head and I knew that she too must be suffering from the intense heat. There were two guards in the room and every so often one would go out and perhaps have a drink. They were determined to keep us uncomfortable.

After quite a long time, Irene came down looking thoroughly exhausted and weary. Together we were given a last chance to admit that we had received news from Mrs Nicolle. We were both silent. Our interrogator was furious and again promised prison and court martial with, this time, four years in a concentration camp. In a way this consoled me because I did not believe that the war would last another four years and I thought this was an idiotic statement to make.

The officer then went over to Mrs Newland. I could not hear what he said but her reply was loud and clear. She asked what was to happen to her invalid husband, as he could not be left alone. His reply was that he would most likely be transferred to a military hospital.

The officer calmed down once more and said that he would make things easier for us if we told the truth. Surely we did not want to give up our lovely home and be sent away? He then had a long discussion with the other man and, with a disgusted look at me, took Mrs Newland upstairs and it started all over again. Then came Irene's turn and finally my own. As I left the room, the man who was staying downstairs was watching Irene and I was able to look at Mrs Newland as I passed her. I felt certain that she was again mouthing the words, 'Ruby confessed.' I felt this time that there was no doubt.

I was once more told to sit in the same place. It was hotter than ever and he went straight to the attack. If I did not tell him about the news that I had received and passed on, within one hour he would show me that I was wrong and it would be no use coming to him afterwards as it would be too late. This time I decided that I would no longer be calm so, by way of a change, not shouting as he was, but loudly, I gave him the same reply as before. He glared at me and then walked up and down the room before talking again with the other man.

Meanwhile, I was thinking about Ruby and what she had told Mrs Newland. Was it another trick? He came over to me and once more said, 'You will see.' Then I went down alone and Irene was sent up again, no doubt to go through the same routine again.

Quite soon Irene was down again, followed by the two men. I felt that it might be over, but it was not. We were told to sit side by side as he read out Mrs Newland's statement. It said that we had received the news from Mrs Nicolle, written on a piece of paper in the mornings but that she had not passed it on to anyone else except her husband. Mrs Newland quickly chimed in to say that it had never been mentioned to anyone else, but she was immediately silenced. I expect that she had spoken to emphasise to us that we should stick to that particular point. Irene and I looked at each other in astonishment.

I must admit that I was absolutely muddled. We had decided amongst ourselves to say nothing. All I could think of was that Ruby had been brought here and confessed in front of Mrs Newland. That seemed the only explanation possible. I looked at Irene but her eyes were closed and we could not speak to each other.

Again I was taken upstairs and the others were left below. I was seated again in the intolerable seat. 'Now,' he said with a sickly smile, 'what is your statement?' I replied that I had nothing to say and that I was absolutely stunned and could not understand what Mrs Newland had been saying. I said it was impossible, of course, and that I did not believe it and did not know what to say. I said I felt hopelessly bewildered and thought it must be some sort of trick. He again threatened me with more of the same treatment but I had it firmly in my head that I must deny having heard or passed on any news, no matter what anyone said.

This interview seemed to take forever, questions and answers following one another until I was in a daze. The horrible man was standing at the window and I was looking at the sea in the distance beyond him. Again he repeated, 'What is your statement?' I glared at him and, in a loud voice, said, 'You have had my answer.' He rose from his chair in an absolute fury and screamed again. (I am fully convinced that to become a member of the Gestapo screaming was an essential qualification, besides being tall, brutal and ruthless. I thought then that they were all cowards and found this easier than going out to fight.)

He flounced out of the room and I followed slowly behind. After he had had a heated talk with one of his colleagues, he turned to Mrs Newland and told her that she could go home and that there was a bus that she would be able to catch. I asked whether we too would soon be able to leave as I had a class of children who would be waiting at the studio. He said that I could send a message by Mrs Newland that there would be no class. She looked very upset and asked if she could stay instead of us as I was busy with the school and should not be upsetting others. But she was again told to go, and warned that if she mentioned anything about the case outside she would quickly find herself in gaol.

She looked so very tired and said, 'Goodbye. It's true.' The men were talking together by now and did not notice her say, 'It's true.' I attempted to smile as she was finally ushered from the room.

They then began to take down my statement. In the light of what I had heard Mrs Newland say, and particularly her last words at the door, I could see that I had to admit that we had received news from Mrs Nicolle, but that we should stress that we had not passed it on. I could not imagine how confused Irene must feel, when faced with our two statements. She had not heard her mother's last words and I had no way of passing the facts on to her, but all she could do was follow our lead.

I believe that the Gestapo had prolonged this interrogation in the hope that they would prise out more names from us and add to their score. Perhaps they hoped to earn a medal!

They followed the same routine with Irene, asking for her age, school, employment etc. and then her statement. She admitted receiving news from Mrs Nicolle, but denied recognising the handwriting or knowing who wrote it or who owned a wireless. She said she had told no-one and knew nothing more.

Our statements were then typed out and we were obliged to sign them. I expected that we would then be allowed to go home for the cup of tea and aspirin that I was longing for. But, to our horror, without another word being spoken to us, we were put into a car and driven to the prison. This day, March 19th 1943, has remained indelibly inscribed on my heart.

CHAPTER FIVE

PRISON: A QUESTION OF SURVIVAL

The car was driven very fast which did not give us much time to talk. I was able to tell Irene that I had gathered from her mother that Ruby had confessed. There was much explaining to be done but it could obviously not be done then. We hoped that we would not be long in prison and that they were only trying to frighten us. We had signed the statements. What more could they want?

When we arrived at the prison we were at once taken into the office. An officer took some items out of Irene's handbag and without a word took her away. I felt very upset at seeing Irene leave the room. Little did I realise that this would be the last time I would see her for three weeks.

In my turn I had to give up my keys, money, pencil and papers which I had in my pockets. I managed to keep my comb and they did not notice my watch which was hidden by my shirt cuff. I was then taken away by a warder and I had difficulty in making him understand that I wanted to go to the lavatory. This was in a dark passage with no light and I was obliged to keep the door open while the warder stood outside.

I was taken down a flagstoned passage to a small cell about eight feet by seven feet with a wooden floor, a heavy iron door, a window that was too high to see out of, a small wooden bench and a pail in the corner. A little metal shelf was fixed to the wall in front of a spy hole to allow the warder to look in. What was to be my bed was a wooden board with two cross pieces which lifted it about six inches off the floor. Later I found that if I turned it on its side I was able to climb on it to peep out of the window, but there was nothing to see except the window of the cell across the yard. The light was controlled from outside. A hot water pipe ran along the wall under the window but it was not hot and I was cold. My head was absolutely splitting. I longed for some food and drink, but nothing came, although it was nearly eight o'clock in the evening, a long time since our lunch at 12.30pm.

I wondered where Irene was and longed for her. She was no doubt in the same sort of cell and she must be hungry too. I felt absolutely miserable.

Suddenly the lights came on and a key was turned in the lock. The warder entered and beckoned to me. I followed him down the passage past about seven other cell doors into a large room where he pointed to a pile of mattresses. I took one and he brought a brown blanket. That was all I was to have on my board. He was quite a little man and unfortunately he spoke only German. He was a rather different type from the 'Silvertide Group' (Silvertide was the Gestapo headquarters in Jersey). I asked for water but he shook his head and led me back to my cell where he locked me in, and soon the lights went out again.

Before I lay down, I shook up the old straw mattress, folded the blanket in half and got in between. Fortunately I had two handkerchiefs. I put one with my scarf under my head and the other over the rug under my chin. I did not want that dirty old rug to touch my skin.

I soon realised that I had stirred up the livestock when I had shaken the mattress. I was bitten all over. I would certainly not do that again. And so I lay there all night, motionless, tormented with so many thoughts pestering my brain. I still had the terrible headache and was so uncomfortable and in the depths of depression. Why had all this happened to us?

At six o'clock the next morning there were loud shouts and the sound of heavy boots in the passageway outside. Keys were turned and eventually it was my turn. I was instructed to take my mattress and blanket back to the room they had come from and to place them on the pile. I realised that I would not have the same ones the following night – or could it possibly mean that I was going to be released? I was allowed to go to the lavatory, again watched by the warder, and then I was told to empty the pail, which I had not used. I was given a broom to sweep my cell and then I was given a bowl of water and a grey towel and told to wash, while two warders waited in the passage.

I counted 12 cells and was able to see that there was a big iron door at one end of the passage and the room where the mattresses were kept at the other. There was a door out of this room but I could not see beyond it.

An officer was yelling at the warders who appeared very much the underlings and never spoke. I was soon locked in my cell again and shortly after this breakfast arrived. It was served in two dirty looking mugs, one with some sort of coffee and the other with some revolting looking porridge. I tried the coffee. Although it was horrible, I was so thirsty that I forced myself to drink about half of it, but I could not attempt the porridge. Even to look at it made me feel ill. There was also a hunk of bread so I just munched that. I can hardly say that it was a delectable breakfast and I was still very hungry.

The noise continued out in the passage. I thought that the prisoners were going through the same routine, one at a time, so that they would not see one another. I was beginning to think that this young officer with all his shouting must be hoping to join the Gestapo, or perhaps it was necessary to shout to be an officer in the German Army. I did not think that I was going to like him. He looked insolent. The two warders were clearly subservient.

Later I heard steps outside in the yard so I turned my sleeping board up on its side against the wall under the window. I was able to climb on it, from where I could reach the bars and pull myself up. I was only able to see part of the yard, so the person walking was only in view for about half a minute. When he came under my window I called out, 'Hello!' but he passed on. I waited until he came into view and then disappeared and again passed beneath my window. As he went by he said, 'Can't stop, the guard is watching!' He did not pass again. It must have been the end of his exercise time. I put my plank down again. If it was known that I had been looking out it would probably be taken away during the daytime.

About fifteen minutes later it was my turn. The warder opened the door and called out, 'Promenade!' I was taken along the passage and through the big door at the end into an office. There were three men in there and they all looked me over. I was new to them. They signalled to the warder to take me through the door and out into the yard. The guard was in and out of the door quite often, but spent most of the time watching me. It was good to get out into the fresh air and I walked quite briskly up and down and then around several times. I gazed at the windows but I did not see any faces. The yard was entirely enclosed with high walls and buildings and looked most forbidding. I was out there for about twelve minutes.

As I came back through the office I said to the officer, 'I want to see my wife.' He glared at me and said, 'Wife, wife!' and pointed to the door. The warder took me back to the cell. On the way back, I took the opportunity to go to the lavatory. The door was, as always, open but I managed to conceal some newspaper in my shirt. There was not much about and it might be needed later.

Quite soon after I got back there were loud shouts, the rattle of keys and the slamming of doors. Finally this commotion stopped right outside my cell and in marched a little aggressive-looking Nazi officer, full of swagger and self-importance. We glared at each other for a minute while the warder stood by the door, looking rather nervous. The officer yelled at the warder and then, without a word to me, marched out again. I never knew what this was about. He went on down the passage, visiting each prisoner. At one cell there was a prolonged exchange of what sounded like swearing. I soon discovered that this man was the terror of the warders and they hated him.

I studied the walls of the cell and wondered who had inhabited it before me. There were no signs on the walls or door but my imagination was running riot.

At last lunch arrived: the same two dirty mugs, one with some watery, tasteless soup with a few pieces of cabbage floating in it, the other with potatoes which were so bad that one just could not eat them. They were accompanied as usual by a hunk of bread.

When the little warder came in I said, 'Potatoes bad!' and made a face. He did not understand English, but he understood my grimace and agreed.

That afternoon I put my head on the wall table on my folded hands and tried to sleep, but sleep would not come. I kept worrying about Irene and how my in-laws would manage with no help from us and no Ruby. They would have our rations but there would be no one to go around to try to find the odd extra thing which I sometimes managed to collect.

At about four o'clock they came for me again for another 'promenade'. I was happy to get out again, for twenty minutes this time, and I was able to use the lavatory, with the door open again, on the way back. Nobody was in sight anywhere.

While I was outside I decided that I must try to do something about exercise when back in my cell. I must keep myself active. I walked up and down in the cell, crossways, toe to heel, but it was such a small space. I did some ballet exercises, but although I managed a few I was very clumsy in my heavy shoes and I dared not try in bare feet because of the splinters. I had no change of socks and did not want to get my socks filthy from the floor. However, I did keep up some movement for a while which was a distraction.

I went over to the door and studied the notice stuck there. I could recognise very few words of the German, but I started to make up words from the letters. If only I had a pencil and paper I would be able to do something to combat the boredom.

Eventually the evening meal arrived, this time with the other warder I had seen. I asked him if he could speak any English or French, and as he did know a very little French, I asked if my wife was in the building. He said that women were in another building, and then he was gone to deliver to the other cells. This meal was again a hunk of bread and two mugs, one with coffee and the other with something that looked like pineapple cubes, but which turned out to be swede. I dislike swede, and the smell was horrible, so once again all I ate was the bread and I drank most of the coffee. I did not care about food. What I wanted to know was, why were we being kept here?

When he returned for the mugs I asked him for paper and pencil. He did not appear to understand but, when I made the action of writing, he shook his head and smiled and said, 'Officier, mal!', and gave himself a slap. He took the mugs and was gone.

I began to think about the school. They would all know by now where we were and some of the classes might be going on. I tried to spend most of the evening thinking about the next production which we had started working on, but it was very difficult to concentrate. I could only think of Irene.

The same warder came to take me to fetch a mattress. I asked him his name. This appeared to please him and he said something that sounded like 'Alti'. When I repeated it he nodded. I think that I must have been one of the first to fetch my mattress that night as there was a much larger pile than the night before. Afterwards I heard more doors being unlocked. I arranged my blanket, scarf and handkerchiefs, at the same time taking care not to disturb the livestock in the mattress. The light had gone out but there was still some light coming through the window and I walked up and down for a while. I was not looking forward to another night on the lumpy recliner.

I kept thinking of Irene and of our marriage. We had only been married three years and our hopes and plans, our ambitions and our expectation of having children had turned into an empty dream. Somehow I found myself under the blanket, but still my mind wandered. How did we ever get ourselves into this position. The wretched Gestapo officer assailed my brain with his 'You will see! You will see!'. I thought I would never get to sleep. I felt as if I had been there for ages, but this was only my second night in prison.

I must have eventually fallen asleep because something woke me: it was the army of livestock attacking my body from below. I was still awake when the first ray of sunshine threw the pattern of the bars on the wall, reminding me of where I was.

What day was it? I decided that I must make some mark on the wall each day, but there was nothing to use. We were not even given any implement to eat with and had to use our fingers.

There were shouts in the passage again, footsteps on the stone floor and keys turning in iron locks. Soon it was my turn and the warder whose name I did not know appeared at the door and I took my mattress and blanket back. Then he brought water and a towel. I washed as best I could. This time he had given me some soap, winking as he handed it over. Perhaps I was not meant to have it. It was unpleasant but better than nothing. When he collected the bowl and towel, he looked around and then handed the soap back to me. I showed him the bites on my chest and he opened his shirt and showed me that he had the same, except that they were worse.

A little later breakfast came. It was exactly the same as the day before. Had I wanted to eat the porridge it would have had to be with my fingers! Later I was able to take my pail out and make the very important visit to the lavatory: I was glad that I had kept that piece of paper. Then the broom arrived. That day I saw nothing of the noisy officer.

Later I thought that I heard walking under my window, so I raised the board against the window and heaved myself up. I waited to see who would pass on the other side of the yard, but it was a German. I was rewarded, though, for I found a useful piece of grit, sharp enough to make the marks I wanted to denote the days. I decided that I would make these marks up there on the window cill where they would not be noticed.

I started on my exercises. I intended to do ten minutes at the end of every hour during the day, which should keep me fit, but I wondered if I would be able to keep it up as I was not eating very much.

I was interrupted for 'Promenade' which I looked forward to, even though it was only a walk in the gloomy yard. This time there was a face at one of the upstairs windows. Someone was waving. I was unable to see who it was but I waved back and he stayed there throughout my walk which lasted about fifteen minutes.

There was a different officer in the little office, so I tried again. 'Could I see my wife?' He shook his head but he said in halting English, 'In the other block.' I felt at last that there was an officer I could communicate with. I asked if it would be possible to write to her but he replied, 'Gestapo not allow!' I hoped that I would be able to see that man again as he might be persuaded to give Irene a message for me. I felt I must try every possible way of making a connection. I did so want to know how she was. I thought, like me, she was probably only eating the bread, which was hardly enough sustenance.

During the morning, I had a very welcome surprise. The officer I had spoken to arrived with a beaming warder, bringing a bag containing my pyjamas, toothbrush etc and a pair of socks and a dressing gown. It may sound trivial but for me it was wonderful to be able to sleep in pyjamas and dressing gown, clean my teeth and change my socks. I wondered how Mrs Newland had managed to do this as she would have had to bring the parcel in herself. The officer let me know that Irene too had had a parcel and I felt so grateful because I knew that she would be equally happy to have these things. I wanted to clean my teeth right away but I had no water. I would have liked to get a pencil and paper but I realised that everything would have been examined before it came through to the cell. Nevertheless I had been been extremely fortunate.

Lunch came, with the same dreary food, but because of my parcel I felt able to tackle the bread and soup with a little more gusto than usual.

A German doctor came to visit me. He spoke a little English and asked if I was well. I said that I was but that I would have liked more edible food and I wanted some water to drink and to brush my teeth. He replied that he was not in a position to carry out prisoners' demands but he would try to get me water. I asked him about my wife and he said that she was well and that she had been able to have some things sent in. From this, I gathered that she must be able to speak to someone more lenient, which was good news. I asked if he would be seeing her again but he said not before the following week. I could not believe that we would be here the following week.

I then went out for my afternoon promenade. The three disagreeable officers were in the little office leading to the yard and so I had no chance of talking to anyone. When I arrived in the yard I was amazed to see another man walking there. He was German but he spoke French. He asked me my room number, which was seven, and said that we would talk some evening. He said that we should not be talking now and he kept shaking his head so that anyone watching would think that he did not understnd me. He moved away and when I had made another round, he was gone. I pondered on what he had said and wondered why he had asked me what my room number was. What was he doing there? It seemed very strange.

For the evening meal there was a dab of butter about the size of a fingernail on the stale bread, otherwise everything was the same as the night before.

I was so glad that that night I could have my pyjamas and dressing gown to separate me from the smelly blanket but, as usual, I delayed going to bed and wished I had more protection from the livestock. I had done quite a lot of exercise and so I hoped to sleep better.

It was about 2am when I heard a lot of noise, the lights came on, the big iron door at the end of the passage was opened and the sound of loud voices and heavy boots echoed down the corridors. The great key turned in a lock some distance away. A loud shouting lasted a few minutes, and then I heard boots marching towards my cell and shouts again as someone fumbled with the lock.

I leapt out of bed as my Gestapo friend from Silvertide marched in with the noisy officer.

'Well, how do you like your new home?' he asked.

I ignored the question.

'Not like your own home!'

'Rather a late call,' I replied.

'Now, will you give me the names of the other people to whom you passed on the news? I know that there are others. Your memory cannot be that bad.'

I could not believe that we were starting with the same stupid questions all over again. I was by now very angry, but I kept myself under control and did not answer. He too was angry and red in the face and he started to yell at me again. He said that the trial would be in a few days' time and that he would suggest a longer period for me in a concentration camp because I had not been willing to co-operate with him. I said that I had signed a statement and that there was nothing more to say. I was more than ready for a court martial. He was now quite mad, his face distorted. Finally he departed after further talk with the officer. I heard him visiting another cell at the end of the passageway. I hoped and prayed that he would not visit Irene at this time of night as it would terrify her. I got back under the blanket, but there was little sleep for me the rest of the night. My thoughts were in a whirl. The Gestapo officer was just trying to wear me out with his tirades.

When Alti came in with my breakfast the following morning, he brought an extra mug with water. He smiled and put his finger to his lips. I understood. I took my mattress back and I saw my French-speaking German prisoner going to his cell. 'Maybe tonight,' he whispered. Here was another mystery.

After my promenade I got busy on my exercises and tried to banish all thoughts of the night before, but I was worried. When I climbed to the window to make my mark for the day, I could see someone walking in the yard and although I did not know him, I realised that he was not German, because if he had been I would have heard the sound of heavy boots. So when he passed under my window I called out but there was no reply. I climbed up to the window quite often in the hope that I might see someone that I knew.

That wretched little Nazi officer was round again. He came twice a day, sometimes visiting a cell and making himself objectionable. He made enough noise to be heard all over the building.

I managed to eat one potato that lunchtime; the others looked horrid as did everything else. In the afternoon, when I went for my promenade, the quiet officer was in the little room next to the yard. I asked him about my wife and he said she was well and that the next time he was in her building he would tell her that I was OK and walking well.

When I came back from the walk he was still there. He told me that Irene had a very good warder and that she had been able to speak on the phone for a minute or two, although this was very dangerous. I thanked him and was ushered back to my cell by Alti.

This was wonderful news. Alti said to me, 'Happy?' Oh yes, I certinly was! At last I had something to alleviate the boredom. I wondered if it was Mrs Newland that had phoned, or if Irene had managed to persuade some officer to let her make a phone call. It would not be my obnoxious little Nazi. I was lucky that both my warders were sympathetic towards me but they were both very frightened of him. I later learned that the name of the second warder was Boris. I did not think that he was German; he was most likely Polish.

I then tackled my exercises with renewed vigour. This was certainly a good tonic. The evening meal was again the same, but with a tiny bit of cheese perched on the hunk of bread. It was so small that I very nearly missed it.

Very soon after the lights went out there was a sharp knock on the door. I at once thought of that man I had seen in the morning. He had been on my mind. I was not certain whether he was French or German. When he spoke I was able to hear him quite clearly, close to the door. He said that he could open the door but he would not do so as he would only have the time it took the warders to unlock the iron door to get back to his own cell.

I was amazed. He told me that both he and his friend were thieves in ordinary life. They had been brought to prison for stealing food from the barges and selling it in St Helier and they were working on a plan of escape, which they did not think would be too difficult. Certainly they believed that the iron door would pose no problem. They had already been in trouble with the Gestapo in France but, with the help of the Underground, they had reached St Malo with new passports. There they had obtained work on the barges.

He asked if I had any food to spare. Like me they were hungry. He told me that there was no food kept in our section of the prison – he had investigated – and that beyond the room where we collected our mattresses there were bathrooms. That was news to me. I was glad to know that there were some in that part of the building and I wondered when we would be able to have a bath. I was longing for one! He was about to tell me something else when he suddenly broke off. He must have heard something.

I was sitting on the stool with my head in my hands, thinking about these men and the extraordinary lives they led, when I heard the iron door being opened and the lights were switched on. I thought, 'Not again!' but yes, it was the Gestapo officer, his voice louder than at any other time. You never heard such screaming! Well, I was learning to take it all in my stride. His constant emotional threats were the expression of an extravagant, obnoxious and loathsome man.

He entered my cell shouting, 'This is your last chance, otherwise it will be concentration camp!' Quietly, I replied, 'I have told you all I know. There is no reason why I should depart from the truth.' He continued angrily that I would suffer in the camp etc etc and most likely never see my home on this lovely Island again. I said, 'I am very cold. I would like to have my overcoat. I would most likely require it in the camp.' This, of course, enraged him all the more and he left, screaming obscenities. I called out, 'Don't forget my overcoat!'

This time I did not feel at all upset by the interview. There was no chance that we should be sent anywhere without a court martial and who could possibly convict us on just receiving news? I believed that he must by then have realised that nothing more could be gained by these interviews. There was, of course, that little uncertainty at the back of my mind, but I kept it well back. The lights went out and I found my way to bed.

The next morning, after my frugal breakfast and the usual domestic duties, I climbed up to the window and made my mark for the day. There was nobody in sight. How dull it all looked. I was thinking again of the visit of the Gestapo officer on the previous night. If he came again I must think of something with which to aggravate him. It was becoming something of a duel between us. He did not worry me any longer and he certainly did not get anything from the interrogations. It was nothing but a bit of play-acting.

This day was to be full of surprises. When I came back from my promenade, Boris was waiting to take me to the bathroom. Oh to have a hot bath! Well, it was not quite hot, but it was nevertheless enjoyable. All too soon Boris unlocked the door and brought me a skimpy towel. As I was being led back to my cell I noticed that there were two little bathrooms. There was a wash basin and a cupboard in the bare rooms but it did not look as though they allowed more than one person in there at a time. It was wonderful to feel clean and fresh and a little more sprightly, so I got down to my exercises with more vim and vigour.

In the afternoon another of the Gestapo men who had been at Silvertide when we were first arrested turned up. Not yelling, but speaking in a loud, harsh voice, he demanded why I had not told the truth to the superior officer. I again went over it all quite calmly, saying that I had nothing more to say as my signed statement was complete.

He said, 'We are not satisfied. You have not told us to whom you passed on the news.' I replied that they had better have proof if they were making such an allegation, but that that was impossible as I had told no-one. He was angry. 'Lies! More lies!' he spat.

I asked him when the Court Martial would be, but there was no reply. He just glared at me and stormed out. He too was a most objectionable creature, but at least he did not shout or scream.

Whenever my spirits rose, something seemed to happen to tear them down again. I enjoyed my next promenade but I was disappointed that the friendly officer was not about and so I had no opportunity to speak to the guards. However, soon after I got back to the cell, my spirits rose again. Alti brought in a bag containing a flask of tea, some sandwiches and little cakes. He stood there watching me with a big smile on his face as I unpacked the parcel. I gave him a little cake and he was so pleased. No-one could imagine how I felt at the sight of the food and drink. It was wonderful, miraculous. I was so hungry that I could have eaten the lot there and then.

I immediately helped myself to my first cup of tea for nearly a week. I decided, however, but with much reluctance, that I had better space out this food as it might be the one and only gift that I received. I remember how difficult it was not to devour the lot. I ate one sandwich and one little cake. They were so good. I looked at the rest longingly, and thought how splendid it was of Mrs Newland to have achieved this. She would have had to get a bus in and out of town and this would have entailed a long wait as they were not frequent. I was amazed that it had been allowed in. I was so thankful. I knew how Irene would be enjoying this. If only we could have been together.

When the evening meal came in I ate the bread with the speck of butter and one potato. I had one sandwich from my own food, but that had to be all. I had one more cup of tea before bed and hoped that I would have a better night, although this largely depended on the enemy in the mattress. There was also always a chance of a visit from the Gestapo. One visit was certainly enough for the day.

By this time there were six marks on my window cill, so it must have been Thursday, March 25th. How much longer would this go on? That night one of the Frenchmen came to my door and told me that he had spoken to a German detainee called Heinrich, who was terribly fed-up with the war. Heinrich worked mostly in the Warden's house. He had switched on the English news while he was stationed at Elizabeth Castle and for this he was put in prison for twelve months. He expected to be sent to Russia after his prison term ended. I found this very depressing news. I wondered if they gave their own people stiffer sentences or if we might face a similar sentence. Apart from that depressing bit of news, Friday was a dull day and I finished the rest of my food.

The next day, Saturday March 27th, another most welcome parcel arrived which included a shirt and underwear. This was wonderful. I did not know how Mrs Newland could manage to find this food for both of us. I thought that some kind person must be helping her because we had so little in the house. After a few minutes Alti came back for the flask so I thought that someone was waiting. I wondered who it was.

Surprisingly, on the following day, a package of small cakes also arrived. As it was a Sunday, I realised that these could not have been brought by Mrs Newland as there was no bus that day. It was great to have help from others.

That evening the Frenchman, whose name was Louis, came to my door again. I had not yet told him why we were in prison. He said that there was another Jerseyman on this floor but that he did not know his name. His cell was too close to the iron door for them to speak to each other because he would not have time to get back to his own cell before the light came on. Louis said that he was trying to persuade his friend to make their escape quite soon and asked if I would like to join them. He was quite certain that he knew how and when to make the attempt. The German who lived in the Warden's house knew the ropes. I said that, as much as I should like to, I could not try to escape as my wife was in the women's block and I could not leave her to the Gestapo.

He told me that he had a girlfriend that he had been sleeping with at St John's and would stay with her until he could make other plans. I must say that I found these evening conversations quite an education. He seemed quite free to move about the building.

The next few days went by with nothing to relieve the boredom. Food continued to flow in from friends which was marvellous, but apart from that all was routine.

It was the following Thursday night that Louis came to the door to say goodbye and we wished each other good luck. They were going to attempt to escape in the early hours. In spite of his lifestyle he seemed quite likeable. It was strange that he should come to say au revoir. I thought he must have a kind heart. Who would believe that I had been consorting with thieves?

The next morning there was a bit of a rumpus. The little Gestapo officer was shouting louder than ever before and it went on and on. I expected that the discovery that two men were missing was going to cause a good deal of trouble in the camp. I hoped that they had got away safely. When Alti came with the breakfast he was looking pretty gloomy. He made a gesture and I knew that the Frenchmen had got away. After my promenade Boris came to fetch me for my second bath. That made my day. I was allowed half an hour in the bathroom and I made the most of it.

On the Saturday afternoon of the second week – April 3rd according to my scratch marks – the officer who had been at the office on the way to the yard and whom I had not seen of late, appeared with another nosebag. Mrs Newland must have been working hard to organise all that food and to have it brought to the prison.

The officer informed me that he had been on duty at the Reception Office and that Mrs Newland had phoned several times wanting to speak to Irene. The last time he had been alone in the room and so had managed to let Irene speak to her mother. I had no doubt that she had been thrilled at this opportunity. Her mother had told her that the Court Martial was to be held on the following Friday and that she would also be in court. There had not been time to say very much as he would not risk letting them talk for long. It was indeed kind of him and very good news. He was not able to tell me anything about the Court Martial. Before parting he gave me a book in English which he must have found in the prison when the Germans took it over. I was overjoyed to have the book. It was turning out to be a very auspicious day.

The only change on the following day was that there must have been a new prisoner brought into a cell above me who was very noisy. I heard a lot of walking up and down which went on for hours. I found it most disturbing. I was glad to have a book to read but I thought that I must read it slowly as I might not manage to get another. I had heard nothing about the escapees and I thought they must have achieved their aim.

The following days went so slowly, all following the same pattern. My mind could not rest. The situation was precarious and the tension gave me a perpetual headache. I wondered what was happening at home, on the Island and in the world at large. I certainly missed hearing the Nine O'Clock News from the BBC. With this in mind I tried to make contact with other prisoners by tapping SOS on the pipes. Perhaps someone in another cell might know the Morse Code, and I thought I remembered most of it from my scouting days. Only once did a sound come back and then it did not mean anything.

On the Wednesday, when Alti brought me a parcel of food and I was handing him a little cake, I noticed that his eyes opened wide when he saw my hard-boiled egg. No doubt he had not seen one for quite some time. I always gave something to whichever warder brought in the food and they always showed that they appreciated this.

Mrs Newland had managed to contact Advocate Valpy to represent us at the trial, and on the Thursday afternoon, April 8th, the day before the trial, Boris escorted me to a small office where Advocate Valpy was seated. Before I had time to shake hands or say, 'Good afternoon' Irene came in. I rushed over and kissed her. I apologised to Advocate Valpy, who understood how we felt. After all, I had not seen Irene for such a long time. She looked thin but well and smart, as she always did, no matter what she was wearing, because she had such a good figure and a good carriage.

How wonderful it was to see her again. Strange as it may seem, no interpreter attended that meeting and the three of us were alone in the room.

Advocate Valpy told us that the trial was to be at 9.15am in one of the rooms at the Royal Court. Eighteen of us were to be tried in connection with the case, including Mrs Newland and Mrs Bathe who were the only two who were not in prison. He did not hold out much hope for us as he said that the German authorities considered us guilty before we were tried. The entire case against us was so paltry that he felt there was very little he could say on our behalf, but he would do his best. We wished him goodbye and he was gone. We had only a minute to ourselves before an officer arrived and we were ordered back to our cells. This was not exactly a comforting interview.

Next morning we were all brought into the garden in front of the women's building. This was the first time that I knew exactly who were the accused besides ourselves, Ruby and her husband. I had not even been aware that so many were involved until Advocate Valpy told us. I now saw Mrs Alexander, Mr Mourant (Secretary of the Hospital) Mr Demery, Mr Stark and Mr Wakeham, all of whom were in the same building as Irene. My block housed Deputy

Mourant, Canon Cohu, Mr Coutanche, Mr Tierney, Mr Nicolle Senior and Jack Nicolle, Mr Lanagan and Mr Downer.

It was interesting to stand there and see all these people come out as their names were called. How they all came to be involved in the case I could not imagine. Irritatingly half a dozen German officers watched to see that we did not speak. We were told that we were to be taken to the Court by bus, and we had to stand there in silence just looking at one another until we were led out to it. It seemed very strange to be riding through the streets of the town after having been shut up all that time. Before arriving at the Court we had our first glimpse of greenery since being imprisoned – the trees in the Parade Gardens.

While we were waiting outside the Court, guarded by German soldiers, we could see people gathering, but we could not speak to anyone. Once we got into the Court we made up for lost time and chattered to each other rapidly. Mrs Newland arrived in the taxi arranged for her by the Gestapo and we were allowed to sit together. Mrs Bathe arrived a little late as her carriage had been late calling for her.

Besides the Gestapo brutes from Silvertide in plain clothes, there were the guards, Herr Teinschnark the interpreter, and Advocate Valpy and Advocate Luce, the latter defending Mr Tierney and Mr Lanagan.

I cannot recall all the details of the trial. Each charge was read out separately, but most of it was repetition and it all took a long time. There was much argument over the unreasonable and in some cases fabricated accusations. Jack Nicolle was presented as the chief 'criminal' because he had had the wireless set and had been caught with it. Mr Tierney was the next because he had written out some leaflets and distributed them. The other people were practically all involved through these two although Ruby had, of course, passed the news to us. Mr Tierney had given the news to Deputy Mourant, Canon Cohu and Mr Coutanche, who had in turn given it to Mr Mourant and Mr Downer, both at the Hospital.

Mrs Bathe had owned the wireless and had had it buried it in her garden. Later she had instructed Mr Demery, her gardener, to dig it up and had loaned it to Jack Nicolle. Mr Demery had afterwards taken the news to Mrs Alexander, Mrs Bathe's companion. Mr Nicolle, Jack's father, had allowed two wireless sets, which had afterwards not worked, to be hidden on his land, and Mr Stark, Jack's uncle, had allowed the good wireless to be hidden on his land after Mr Tierney had been arrested.

Mr Lanagan was involved because when he went to wind up Mrs Bathe's clocks (he was a clock-mender) he told her the news. Mr Wakeham was connected because he used to listen in at Jack Nicolle's house every morning and evening on his way to and from work.

Advocate Valpy spoke very well for us, considering that there was so little for him to work on. We were accused of not giving up the leaflets which Ruby had brought and also of spreading the news. They could not prove the latter and Ruby said that she had burned the leaflets. Mrs Newland was accused of telling the news to her husband! The whole thing was just ridiculous.

At midday we had a short break but were obliged to remain silent. Later on, while the judges were considering their verdict, we were able to talk to one another, and did we talk! We were then allowed out into a hallway and it seems that by this time the guards must have got a little slack because two friends wangled their way in by saying that they were our cousins.

After a while we were ushered back into the Court to hear the sentences which were as follows:

Jack Nicolle	3 years
Mr Tierney	2 years
Canon Cohu	18 months
Ruby Nicolle	8 months
Mrs Bathe	6 months
Mr Demery	3 months
Mr Nicolle Senior, Mr Stark, Mrs Newland, Irene and I	2 months
Deputy Mourant, Mr Lanagan, Mr Coutanche, Mr Mourant, Mr Wakeham	5 weeks
Mrs Alexander	3 weeks

Mrs Bathe and Mrs Newland were told to go home. They would serve their sentences after the Occupation was over as the Civil Prison where they should have been detained was full to capacity.

When we came out of the Court there were large crowds in the Royal Square, waiting to hear the result of the trial. The military police and Jersey civil police were there keeping order. We were all very excited and we got back into the bus amidst cheering and waving. I think that we must all have had headaches because it was past three o'clock and we had had no food or drink since early morning, but that did not stop us from talking.

We did not see Mrs Newland again after the sentences were read out as she had been sent home, but we thought that she had not been looking very well. She had lost weight with worry and she had told us that her husband had lost two stone since the beginning of the Occupation. Of course we had all lost weight but not as much as that.

When I finally got back to my cell, Boris brought me some soup and bread. It was good of him to have arranged for us to have something to eat on our return.

It was a great load off our minds to know at last where we stood, and to expect that there would be no more harassment from that obnoxious little man. However poor our environment might be, nothing mattered any more. We were just so happy that the trial was over and that we could look forward with positive and joyful anticipation to resuming our routines. It had been an amazing experience.

Later that evening there was quite a commotion. I wondered what was going on. Had more prisoners arrived so that people were being moved around? I knew that all the cells in this block were already occupied.

I slept better that night and I felt the tension slowly ebbing from my body. I had spent the evening with my mind filled with so many things that I wanted to know. I was now finding it difficult to curb my excitement.

The next morning when Alti came to my cell I asked what had been happening during the night. He understood my question and I guessed from his gestures that two men were being put into one cell, although I could not be sure. When I went for the morning promenade there was a very fierce-looking officer in the guardroom whom I had not seen before. I had half an hour in the yard in lovely sunshine, which was great.

The days drifted on slowly. I did my exercises and my mind was constantly active with plans for the school and for our home life.

It was the following Wednesday before anything new took place. The rather kind officer came in and told me that my sentence was to be reduced by two weeks, because of the time I had spent in prison before the trial. That was good news, although we had actually done three weeks. The next item of news was that because the cells were all full and they had more prisoners arriving on the following day, we would have to be two to a cell. He thought that I would probably prefer to share with someone involved in my own 'case'. I thought that this must have been the commotion which we had heard the night before. I was jubilant about the two weeks, but a little uncertain about sharing a cell.

Soon after that a bag of food and clean underclothes arrived. I gave Alti his cake. I felt sorry for my warders. I do not think that they wanted any part of this war and they hated the officer in charge of the floor. They were both quiet and polite and there was no roughness in them.

On the Friday afternoon, after I had swept out my room, the Nazi officer arrived and signalled to me to take my things with me. I was taken along to the first cell and found myself being housed with Deputy Mourant. This was lucky as I did know him fairly well. He was quite surprised as he had not been told beforehand that he would have to share his cell. However, after the preliminaries were over we could not stop talking. We got on very well and shared all our food and drink. Deputy Mourant had several books but we had so much to talk about that little reading got done.

I think it was about two in the morning when I was awakened by a loud shout. Deputy Mourant was having a nightmare. The shout was followed by lots of mutterings and then he reached the climax, shouting, 'Sink the bloody ships!' This he repeated several times and then he was quiet. In the morning I told him what he had been trying to do during the night and asked him if he had managed to sink all the ships. He apologised for disturbing me and we had a good laugh about it, but he said it might happen again because, when his mind was overactive, he was given to having nightmares.

Anyway we were in agreement about sinking the ships, given the chance. It was a job I would have relished.

That day we had our promenade together. We walked briskly up and down the yard for half an hour. Though Deputy Mourant was much older than me, we enjoyed each other's company and had much of interest to discuss. As a Member of the States he had been used to being very busy and he must have found his present situation unreal.

The Occupation cannot have been at all easy for any member of the States, although for some, acquiescence to the occupying authorities was an easy way out. He did not want to discuss that, however, but was most concerned about shortages of food and clothing and a feeling of uneasiness among the Islanders.

On a more personal level, he did express his appreciation of what I had been doing to help to keep up the morale of the younger people and he wondered how I would manage to cope with the constant increase in the number of students wanting to join the school. I replied that it was not possible to increase the numbers in any production and that there would be students who would have to wait their turn. I had been thinking of staging smaller shows in some of the parishes in which a few of the beginners could appear, but it was going to be a problem.

That night we were sinking the ships again. I wondered if it was to be a nightly occurrence. It was rather amusing and it did not worry me as I soon went back to sleep.

The next Saturday proved to be full of excitement. All the prisoners in our building were told to collect their belongings and come to the front office. With immense curiosity we hurried to join the others, and then stood around jabbering in terrific suspense for quite some time.

We were not told to go home, unfortunately, but we were all to be moved into the Civil Prison because a large group of prisoners had arrived and needed to be housed in the military wing.

The rest of our group reached the new quarters ahead of us. We were again to be two to a cell and I was pleased that I was still to be sharing with Deputy

Mourant. The accommodation in this part of the prison was very much better. We each had a kind of bunk-bed and there was a table, two stools and a fireplace, though no fire, of course. There was a large window through which we could see people coming and going to the Military Prison. This was much better and we felt sure now that we should survive.

We had three additions to the 'St Saviour Wireless Case', as I later discovered the *Evening Post* called it – Reverend Mr Mylne, his wife and his daughter, who had been detained before us. They were in for the same thing as Irene and I, but had been given longer sentences. Mrs Alexander had been sent home as she became too ill to be kept in prison.

The political prisoners were all allowed out to exercise together and although the yard where we were expected to exercise was too small and we were not able to move very quickly, Irene and I were happy to be together and we were able to exchange our news. Irene was sharing a cell with Ruby and she saw a lot of Mrs Mylne and her daughter who were next door. It had been Mrs Mylne's birthday recently and she had received masses of flowers. She had brought some in to welcome Irene to 'the Newgate Department' as she called it (this part of the prison, the old Debtors Prison, was in Newgate Street). When Mrs Newland found out that we were in the Civil quarters, she sent in some cutlery and a tablecloth with the food. We felt that we were now living in the lap of luxury.

We had a service in the little chapel on the Sunday and again on Good Friday. These services were taken by Reverend Quarrie who came to visit us on several occasions.

We had other visitors during the week, including Mr Crill of the Prison Board who asked us if there was anything he could do for us. We had heard that they did not treat political prisoners too well and we were afraid that they might stop the food from coming in. According to the Matron no-one liked the Prison Governor, but he had been warned, I think by the Board, that we were not to be treated like criminals. Mr Crill was keeping an eye on things and making certain that everything possible was being done for us. Dr Bentlif also came to see that we were in good health and stayed for a chat.

Irene's cell was on the ground floor and she and the Mylnes were in and out of each other's rooms as their doors were only locked after the evening meal. Reverend Mr Mylne who was next door to us was allowed to join them after morning and evening exercise, but there was no such luck for me.

The Under-Matron downstairs was quite a character. She loved to gossip and always waylaid us with some wild and funny stories. This was quite a different situation and we were met with kindness by everyone, but we could see from our window that some women were doing hard labour, dressed in drab grey uniforms, black stockings and clogs. We could not see any men in similar circumstances.

From her window Irene was able to see who brought food for us, although she could not make contact with them as she was too far away. Her mother came twice and she also saw Mrs Allport, the Slades, Mrs Hibbs and my father. The Slades owned a bus company and sometimes their driver brought things from them or from Mrs Newland. Everyone was extremely kind and we had plenty of books. We wished we had had these earlier.

Deputy Mourant continued to 'sink the bloody ships' every night but this did not stop us from enjoying each other's company. It might have been difficult if we had not got on so well.

Irene told me what Ruby had said about her arrest. She said that she had been questioned at Silvertide about taking the news to us at Terra Nova. She denied it: they did not believe her and said that they had both Mr and Mrs Newland in prison but that they would be released if she told the truth. This was why she had made her statement admitting that she had told us the news. But we did not believe Ruby's story – it was extremely doubtful.

When at last we were told that we were to be let out at 7pm on the following Saturday, April 28th, we could hardly believe that the dreadful experience was almost over. Although we had had our sentence reduced by two weeks to six weeks, we had done two days over that time in any case.

When the Saturday came we were so impatient to be off that it became difficult not to show too much excitement in front of those who had to stay there. The Mylnes still had another two months to do. During the afternoon exercise period we said our goodbyes to the others.

The last half-hour was the longest of all. I had everything ready, although, of course, this was very little. At the last moment I said goodbye to the Mylnes. The two Matrons came to the gate to wave farewell to those who were departing but we could not see any of the remaining St Saviour's group as they were not allowed to have their doors unlocked. We thought this pretty mean of the Prison Governor.

When we arrived at the street gate into Gloucester Street, the Jersey Police were there. The whole street had been cleared but crowds had gathered at both ends, not knowing which way we would come. The authorities had feared a demonstration and it might have happened if the two groups had been able to join forces at the gates.

Irene and I were put into a taxi and driven past a cheering crowd at the Parade end of the street and on to our studio. I do not know why but the taximan slowed down as we passed the crowd. I expect it was to enable us to wave.

When we arrived at the studio we found a large party in progress, celebrating our release. Irene was presented with a lovely bouquet from the school as well as other gifts of flowers from many people. They had hoped that we would stay but we had the taxi waiting and we soon departed. We were longing to get home.

We arrived home at 8pm. Mr and Mrs Newland and my aunt were there to welcome us, and Mrs Newland had prepared a simple meal to celebrate. For us, after our harrowing experience, it was a feast.

Mercifully, our ordeal was over. What purpose had it served? Absolutely none, as far as we could see. In retrospect all the intense interrogations and punishment meeted out to us and the other political prisoners, for simply listening to wireless words from one's own countrymen, was out of all proportion for such a trivial offence. But, the Germans at this point were so ruthless and confident of winning the war that even though the prisons were full, some political prisoners like dear old Mrs Bathe and Mrs Newland would have to serve their term after all the hostilities had ended.

We couldn't help but be extremely thankful that for us this ghastly time had ended, though of course, those feelings of helplessness and fear we had had to endure remained with us as an appalling memory.

CHAPTER SIX

LIVING DANGEROUSLY

On Sunday morning we awoke from a long sleep in the comfort of our own bed feeling euphoric and relaxed. It was a lovely day and we hastened out into the garden led by Timmy bouncing ahead, then rushing back to jump up at me, full of enthusiasm. There was a slight breeze, just enough to make the foliage tremble, and with the daffodils dancing below it was a lovely sight and everything was so green. Even our blackbird was there watching us. When we had left here to go to Silvertide and on to our own dreary and uncomfortable prison abode it had been winter.

We lingered over breakfast, and for the time being all talk of prison life was banned: on this we were all in agreement. However, I had to compliment Mrs Newland on the way she had managed to get food to the prison, a magnificent job which did so much to alleviate our situation. She said that everyone had been simply wonderful, helping in any way they could. The Slades had got their bus driver to take the things into the prison when there was no-one else going.

I must say that we had all lost weight. I was particularly worried about Mr Newland as he had lost far more than any of us and his face was drawn. With this in mind, I set off early on Monday morning to visit my farmers. All three were glad to know that we were safely back. I was lucky enough to obtain a little extra milk from each of them and a little butter from one of them with the promise of some eggs at the end of the week. Most of the time I would be able to receive a little extra milk each day. But as they did get frequent visits from the Nazis, it was all becoming more and more difficult. However, I knew that I could rely on their help with whatever they could manage.

I went into the studio to see Mary Burger and find out how everything was going with her elocution classes, and then I had an after-school children's class. The studio was still filled with flowers and there was a little box containing many cards and welcome notes from the students, all very gratifying indeed. News had got around very quickly; there were no absentees from the first class on my return.

As I cycled home there were many planes flying high in the sky and shortly after I heard the bombardment. I think that our planes must have been bombing Cherbourg. There was great excitement here. Cars were dashing about and after dark there were troop movements; searchlights were trying to locate planes and some ack-ack guns were in action. This certainly made me feel part of the scene once again.

We had a little debate as to whether we should risk listening to the wireless news at nine. The German soldiers were all too busy with the night's overhead activity. Mr Newland said he thought that after what we had experienced we would not care for a second innings, but he would not be the one to hold back if we three were in favour. Irene was silent for a moment or so and said: 'While I was in prison I kept wishing for the news. Now to go through it again would be insane.' A moment later she said, 'Why not get it out and forget all that is past?' Our desire for news would override all our past misery. Meanwhile Mrs Newland, who had been playing cards, said: 'I so look forward to nine o'clock. It's truly the best part of the day. You had better hurry – it's nearly ten to nine.'

It was pretty obvious we all wanted that news – our life-line – so we might as well continue to live dangerously, just as we had done before. I then took Timmy on his lead and my little flashlight which I saved for this operation. Timmy had learnt his job. He sat next to me while I raised the wireless from its hole in the ground. He would have known at once if anyone was around. We always walked around the garden before collecting the set, and before returning it to its hideout. I always took it upstairs to the large cupboard under a small staircase at the end of the house that went to the attic. It was safer there if anyone should come to the door while we were listening.

I very much doubted that the Gestapo would want to search this house as they already knew that we had been receiving news from others who were now imprisoned. There were more fields for them to conquer. However, one of us always stayed downstairs just in case of emergency. I volunteered to do this night's watch. The others trooped upstairs for their quiet listen-in. The main news had been that our planes were busy bombing the Channel ports. When Irene came down she was radiant and very happy to be able to hear the BBC News once again.

Now that we were back home I had to attend to the house requirements and try to find a way of supplementing the food ration. There was nothing in the garden ready for the table and the weekly ration was so poor I would be obliged to visit more farms. So far I had refrained from seeking help from any of my students who had farm connections, but the sight of Mr Newland's condition made me feel quite desperate. I would have to explore any possibilities. I had the promise of eggs at the end of the week but must continue to try for veg and anything else.

I had been finding it rather difficult to get on with the various classes during the week. Most of my students were so eager for first-hand knowledge of prison life and the Gestapo, and I in my turn wished for news of what had been happening while we were in jail.

I gathered that the Martello Tower at Bel Royal had been torn down. That was a shame as it was part of the Island's history. A submarine net which could be winched up to let the barges enter had been spread across the harbour – such great expectations! Also, Victoria College was open once more and the boys were all happy to be back, with one rather sad feeling of discontent: the cricket field had now been turned into allotments. The Jersey Ladies College was now a hospital; that must have been quite a transformation for the interior of the building.

The Germans were helping themselves to the wireless sets that we had been obliged to turn in, supposedly for safe keeping, and which would be returned after the war. The many requisitioned cars were now on their way to France by ship. Parts from the now very dilapidated cars parked in the grounds of Springfield were also shipped away.

It was going to be all horses very soon in Jersey, except maybe for the trains. They were running from Gorey to St Helier, just like the old days but not quite the same route. They now ran along the top of the pier. The Island was covered with a network of rail tracks. A photo from the air would certainly have shown the vast changes which had occurred on the Island.

One of my students brought news that a large excavation was being dug in the parish of St Lawrence by prisoners brought over from France. More and more arrived to assist in digging what turned out to be a massive network of tunnels: Russians, Spanish Republicans and later Alsatian Jews, Poles and north Africans – a vast army of men, mostly underfed and working in shocking conditions. I wondered just how many thousands there were, and what the tunnels were going to be used for. I could only guess that they were to become air-raid shelters to protect vast quantities of stores and equipment. No doubt we would learn more at a later date.

Two elderly citizens who had been caught distributing leaflets were given severe prison sentences, but because of their age the sentence was deferred until the war was over. Unfortunately a lady from St Lawrence was not so lucky: she was sentenced to three months for the same offence.

The Germans combed the Island's Museum for possible loot, but some of the valuable objects had already been hidden in a safe place at the beginning of the Occupation.

A disaster took place off Noirmont, one of many around this part of the coast. A ship skippered by a Dutch captain left for Holland with three hundred and seventy passengers, mostly soldiers returning home on leave. Unfortunately the ship struck the rocks south-west of Noirmont. Rescue boats were sent out but only forty-five were saved. The bodies that were washed ashore were buried in St Brelades Cemetery, where there were already many German graves. Around this time some airmen also came down, but we didn't know everything that happened around our coasts.

When I called to see my father he told me a story about a friend of his who like him was a very keen gardener. This friend had various tubs of flowers made from old wine casks: one each side of the door and others scattered round a particular part of the garden. He had fixed a false bottom in one of them. It was quite a simple affair. All you did was to lift off the top half containing a beautiful display of plants when you wanted to retrieve the wireless concealed below.

Apparently, when the Gestapo had unsuccessfully searched the house for the wireless they were most annoyed and insisted on being told where it was hidden: they knew that he had one. He boldly replied: 'You have searched the place thoroughly and found nothing just as I told you. I have no wireless.' Meanwhile the lady of the house was watering the flowers in the tubs including the ones at the door, and when the Gestapo finally came to depart one of the officers actually picked a flower off the very tub where the wireless was concealed.

The death of Mrs Gordon Bennett who had been a great friend of ours was indeed sad news. She was one of the oldest members of the Jersey Green Room Club, a very active member both as actress and producer. We were both very fond of her and were always delighted with her effervescent company. I personally would miss her constant encouragement.

Before the prison adventure I had been working on plans for presenting *Rio Rita*. The script, designs for costumes and scenery were now finished. Mr Walter d'Alcorn, who had always been interested in my theatrical work, promised to help and so I asked him to direct as I would be busy with choreography and everything else. It was great to have him take on this rather formidable production. The Opera House was booked for the week beginning August 21st and so much had to be done. 'Time and Tide wait for no man.'

Most of the vegetables brought onto the Island were commandeered by the Germans. This year's potato crop was a small one. As we did not have many ourselves, we had hoped that we could easily purchase more in order to keep some for seed. We went in for green veg and quite a lot of sugar-beet from which we made syrup. We also dried sugar-beet to make coffee substitute. This was quite a long process in both cases. Unfortunately we lost quite a lot of early fruit: it was out of sight of the house and thus easily stolen. Timmy was not always on watch, preferring to be in our company. However, he did react and recognised the sound of the Germans' heavy boots. If he was outside he followed at a short distance, barking continuously until they were off the property.

Planes often flew near and over the Island; sometimes they were fired on but usually without success. My thoughts and wishes winged their way along with them. It only made me feel more useless than ever being cooped up on the Island. When would we ever get out of here? It had been well over three years.

Fauvic has become a favoured escape point. There appear to be many willing helpers prepared to take the risk. The German authorities have been forced to take stricter enforcement measures.

One of my students who came from the Parish of Trinity informed me that the German Army had taken over and pulled down three farms, the houses, sheds, stables, all buildings and hedgerows. His family were extremely worried as their home was very close to the farmland and no-one knew why they were doing this. It must have been very distressing.

Here are a few more items which helped to alleviate the rather dismal news in the *Evening Post.* For sale: Watering can and Beecham's Pills. For exchange: Poultry food for good dog; Thermos flask for floor polish; Earring sleepers for half dozen cups and saucers. Wanted: One stable broom. Galvanised bath for what? What offers for 28 Beecham's Pills and 12 Carter's Little Liver Pills, also one large Bachin [large brass preserving pan] in good condition?

Children were asked to collect acorns for which they were paid a small sum. Apart from feeding the acorns to pigs, people also made some kind of coffee out of them! We never liked it and had more success making tea with dried blackberry leaves. This meant that the fireplace in our dining room was in constant use as we more or less did all the cooking there and of course it was the only place that was warm. Consequently we used an enormous amount of wood and Irene and I spent our spare time wooding.

A lorry fully laden with Germans went over the cliff at Bonne Nuit and more than twenty men died. This was not the first time such a disaster had occurred, but of course the Germans always tried to keep secret such incidents.

The burial of an American airman named Paitras at Mont à l'Abbé was supposed to be held without publicity. A Catholic service and burial was led by Father Arscott and attended by the Bailiff, the Attorney-General and Dr Shone. Wreaths were laid by the States and by the German Air Force. The grave had been dug earlier that day, but when it was uncovered a red, white and blue wreath was discovered in the bottom of the grave. Someone had obviously broken through the 'no publicity' curtain!

We had one particular item of good luck. One of my good farmer friends promised me two ducks out of his fourteen little ducklings which had just arrived. However, I would have to wait until they were a little older before I could have them. It was going to be a job keeping them from being stolen. I was also going to have to find bedding for them – most likely it would be bracken.

The electricity was now reduced to four units per household, which was very little, and the use of electric refrigerators was prohibited until April 1944! There was nothing much to keep in them anyway. But it was difficult to understand just why until that date. What would happen then?

Half a hundredweight of wood was to be allowed for the month. If we had been obliged to depend on that we surely would have suffered.

One morning there was a great deal of excitement in and around the Ritz Hotel where some of the troops were billeted. It was almost certainly news of the defeat of the Germans in Tunisia. Some of them were shouting insults about Hitler and his picture was thrown out of the window. Quite a fight was in progress when the military police arrived to restore some kind of order. According to people living nearby the fierce fighting went on for some time. We could do with a few more of these disturbances. We were even beginning to hear that some troops were deserting.

Bank managers have been obliged to open their safes' deposit boxes to be inspected by German officials. Nothing was taken there and then, but a note was made of the various valuables, uncut diamonds, gold and securities belonging to local residents.

A young boy was killed when he was knocked down by a car driven by an Irishman who was apparently under the influence of alcohol. We understood that he might not be charged by the local authorities because he was employed by the Germans. We waited to see what the outcome would be.

I was always on the look-out for Allied aircraft and I was one day rewarded when two British fighters and a bomber swept over the Island at terrific speed, shooting up some machine-gun emplacements. The Germans sent up a barrage without success, but in their excitement they even fired on one of their own planes which was in hot pursuit. Although it was quite a way off it was nevertheless exhilarating to watch.

On August 20th 1943 *Rio Rita* opened as planned and to a most receptive audience. I must say that the costumes and sets looked splendid, surpassing all my wildest expectations. We had been fortunate in receiving such wonderful help. Many gifts of lovely shawls, skirts and evening gowns, lace curtains and a tremendous number of useful items had all enabled Madame Blondeau to create stunning costumes.

I had also made frames for the mantillas (large Mexican veils) and this is where some of the lace curtains were used to advantage. The boys who wore strange hats and sombreros did a great job in making them out of cardboard and painting them a shining black. Altogether the entire effect brought overwhelming admiration.

Mazel Slade had the title role – her first big part. She looked marvellous and

sang very well. Tim Feltham was excellent in the male lead – he looked perfect as the Texas ranger. Bert Hibbs joined us once again and was cast as General Estaban which he played with great style. I had included a song especially for him which also became an ideal opportunity for Irene as Violetta. We had been fortunate to have good singers to augment our chorus of Texas rangers.

I had written into my script several small parts to give encouragement to some of the students who showed signs of doing well. In the paperback edition of the book from which I had managed to make up my script, Chick Bean, played by John Le Sueur, was expected to arrive for a meeting with the lawyer (that was me) on a motor cycle (these were both light-comedy roles). This was of course out of the question, so I decided that he should meet me on horseback. The horse was kindly lent by Mrs Stella Dean. John was not keen to ride, but I felt that the horse would add to the production and so we changed the lines around and *I* made the entrance on the horse. Happily the horse behaved perfectly at every performance. From that saddle the orchestra pit looked a long way down.

The *Evening Post* described *Rio Rita* as a 'great success' and said that seldom had a production on the local stage received such a spontaneous ovation as was accorded this one on an opening night. The newspaper treated us well with two separate write-ups. News spread very quickly around the town that we had a live horse on stage (he had not qualified for a mention in the write-up).

Shortly after this production I received a Red Cross letter from my brother mailed from Sierra Leone on November 5th 1942, stamped at some unknown place on January 7th 1943. It had taken nearly a year in transit. It was good news, but he still had not heard from us.

Salt water for cooking purposes was now obtainable from tanks in various parts of the town. As we did not live too far from the sea we went down to the harbour at Gorey and, on showing a special permit, we were allowed to fill our containers with salt water at the slipway. In order to facilitate hauling them up the hill to our house we pressed into use our large hamper on wheels which was normally used in the garden. Even so it was an exhausting job. The salt water had then to be rendered down in a frying pan over the wood fire. Mr Newland was the stoker and this kept him quite busy as much frying had to be done to evaporate the water.

The two ducks which had been promised finally arrived, together with a sack of food – absolutely wonderful. They were comfortably housed in what was normally the coal bunker. Timmy had to be trained to watch over them and not chase them when they were let out into the garden. Irene decided to call one

Facing page: Principals of 'Rio Rita'. *Top: Tim Feltham and Irene Newland*
Bottom: Mazel Slade and Bert Hibbs

Happy and the other Rio Rita. We looked forward to the time when they would produce eggs. They were rather fun to watch, far more entertaining than chickens. If any strangers appeared they would make quite a noise.

We received news from friends at St Clement's about a barge having foundered off the rocks outside the bay. At low tide many of the locals had been out to investigate and had come home with flour, cheese, onions and cognac. I wondered at the time how they had dared to go out. I thought that the beaches were mined, but perhaps the Germans thought it was too rocky for any landing to take place. All such activity was very quickly stopped when the troops arrived. It was hard to understand why they did not try to salvage the cargo immediately. The houses around the Parish were subsequently searched for the goods that had been collected.

A considerable quantity of cement had arrived for more and more fortifications and we heard that a Frenchman was killed during the unloading. Invasion tactics were also practised at the harbour, most likely due to the fact that Britain was bombing the French Channel ports. Could the Germans possibly be thinking that Jersey might be invaded? Just more childish reaction.

There had recently been a number of serious accidents involving children playing with detonators which they found mainly on the beaches. Three little boys were badly injured, one of them having three finger-tips blown off. Sadly on another occasion a small boy was killed. Young people would play with these things, oblivious of the danger involved.

We went through a barrage-balloon period. Many Islanders were intrigued to see more and more ships, cargo vessels and barges arriving in the harbour flying a balloon. One balloon, originally attached to a freighter, broke its moorings and, much to everyone's amusement, floated leisurely over the Island.

Later in the year we were infuriated to learn that a German hospital ship which had arrived in the harbour under escort was seen unloading ammunition, contrary to the Geneva Convention. How low could they stoop? However, we were delighted by the news that Mussolini had resigned. We now waited impatiently for the end of Hitler.

On October 25 the Green Room Club became most adventurous and made theatrical history with an all-Jersey production of an entirely new light opera entitled *The Paladins*. The music was composed by M P G Labalestier, book and lyrics were by Mr H Wyatt and it was produced by Mr Max Le Feuvre. The story was an adaptation of an account of the legends of Charlemagne by a late 15th century Italian court poet, Ausoto.

The production received great acclaim and the Opera House filled rapidly for the entire week. The excellent orchestra was conducted by the composer and the singing was of the very best. Miss Beryl Jorden and Mr H E Godbolt in the leading roles certainly made a great success of their parts and they were well backed up by an exceedingly good cast.

I was asked to put on a special charity show at West's Cinema. The stage was very wide but shallow which caused some concern. However, it did give the opportunity for some of my students who had not been able to do much previously.

A number of white Russians and a very untidy group of Italian troops arrived on the Island, the latter complete with their own band which was playing as they marched up the pier. However, the Germans took very little notice of them.

One day I had news from some of the boys in one of my classes that there had been a call-up for some of the male teenagers. They had to attend College House to have their jobs explained to them. Some were told to pack their bags and be ready to go abroad to work for the Germans. However, many refused but could not be put in jail as there was no room. I found the whole thing rather strange as they were bringing over Senegalese to work here. Why send our men away? The Germans were seeking interpreters for outside as well as clerical work, offering good wages and increased rations. I hoped that they would not reach the stage of compelling Islanders to work for them.

CHAPTER SEVEN

A LITTLE EXCITEMENT

Late one afternoon I had a phone call from some friends to say that they had some good quality and inexpensive material that they did not require. I knew that the word 'material' stood for meat of some kind. These little descriptive words were an arrangement that we had among friends. I had a class that evening and as Irene was in bed with a bad cold, it meant that I would have to go and come back before curfew. I asked them if their old bed had been repaired as I knew someone who would like it. In other words, could I stay the night? We did not want to miss whatever they had.

It turned out to be quite an exciting night. I arrived there just before the nine o'clock deadline, and could not have been there more than three or four minutes when a loud knock sounded on the front door. There were car lights which obviously must be German. My immediate thought was that I had been followed. Mrs Martin rushed to the kitchen and I into the downstairs bathroom: if it was one of my Gestapo friends that I had previously encountered it might cause difficulties. Although one could visit for two days without registering, I did not want to place the Martins in an awkward position.

Finally Mr Martin went to the door. There were two officers. One remained standing beside the car, which now had its hooded lights extinguished. The other at the door demanded to see the cars. Mr Martin replied: 'You have both my cars.' They would not accept the statement and insisted that Mr Martin went out and unlocked the garage and outbuilding. He did not take a light but they were fully equipped. Meanwhile I took advantage of the situation and disappeared into the wooded garden in case they searched the house.

There was nothing to be seen in the garage and outbuilding except the bicycles, including mine. These they examined but all were in a pretty deplorable state. They then cast their eyes over the tractor in one of the sheds and rattled the empty petrol cans. Apparently that was all they were after and they did not enter the house.

Mrs Martin had hurriedly hidden the material (pork) under the wood in a large log basket which was beside the stove in the kitchen. If they had entered and searched the house this would not have withstood thorough scrutiny. But it was cars they wanted. For all of us it was a frightening experience as we felt certain that they would want to search the house. The Martins also had a radio and two guns well hidden.

After the Germans had gone Mrs Martin was very shaken: they had not had such a visit before. Mr Martin produced a bottle of brandy. As this was a very special occasion we should all have a little nip. Mrs Martin said, 'If this continues we will want more bottles before the end of the war.'

The next morning I rode home on my old bike, the 'bounty' well covered with lots of green rabbit food which I had collected before starting, even though I no longer had rabbits to feed. Fortunately this happened before we heard that bicycles with baskets were now being stopped and searched.

When I arrived home I called everyone to the kitchen table to view the unpacking of the bounty, six pounds of gorgeous pork. Of course I knew what the package contained, but it was still quite easy for me to join in the mild state of euphoria. It was some time since we had had such a lovely piece of pork and we were immensely grateful to our friends. We stood there transfixed. Mr Newland roused us into action saying that he was ready to sample some of this windfall without delay. Shortly after this we were told that several farmers in St Martin's had been fined for keeping unregistered pigs.

Wood was becoming a problem as the felling of trees was now forbidden. I was obliged to find a farmer who had a good store and would be willing to part with and transport small logs for our fireplace. This I would be unable to manage with my poor overworked cycle, not to mention the seat of my trousers.

Electricity was another mounting problem. It was often turned off without warning. The Green Room Club was running a play at the Opera House when the place was suddenly plunged into darkness for over half an hour. However, they had anticipated that this might happen. Emergency plans were put into action and the play was able to continue. The latest official announcement stated that electricity would be cut off from 1pm to 7pm, but this really meant nothing as it could be shut off at any time.

There were several escape attempts from the Island around this time and I believe that some met with disaster – too bad after so much preparation for such a great effort. The weather had been pretty stormy. Some of the barges in the harbour sank and lines and trees came down. Unfortunately none came down in our area – they would have provided much-needed fuel.

Civil guards were now stationed at St Clement's Parish Hall and at 'Beauvoir', St Saviour to see that no-one stole the grapes, which were a perquisite of the Feld Kommandant.

A pretty stormy meeting took place between Dr Casper from the German Agricultural Ministry and our own President of Essential Commodities. It had been understood for some time that the bread ration would have to be cut as the wheat crop, which came from Tunisia via France, was no longer available, and our own crop was inadequate.

On top of this, however, and using the recent RAF raid on German ships as an excuse, the Germans were now demanding that all other rations should be cut as well, notwithstanding the fact that the bulk of these were produced locally. Our German friends reluctantly climbed down after the Bailiff handed a letter to the Kommandant to be forwarded to the Protecting Power, pointing out that the inhabitants would be made victims of retaliation for an act of legitimate warfare. So for the moment only the bread ration was cut.

The Germans were getting increasingly fed up with the war. Many who were due to go on leave nevertheless asked to remain on the Island as their homes, villages and towns no longer existed. Others tried to get hold of civilian clothes in the hope that, when the final day came – or even before that – they would be able to become part of the Island community. One soldier who shot an officer tried to obtain a suit of clothes in La Rocque but was later found out and executed. There was quite a spirit of defeatism amongst the guards in some of the German camps.

There was another order concerning tobacco. The German authorities required people who had grown tobacco during 1943 to send in a return. Mr Newland said that it was a laugh. He smoked his as fast as it grew. The leaves went into a frying pan to dry off as he could not wait for them to dry in the usual fashion.

There had been tremendous bombing over St Malo of late and a heavy barrage was put up as the planes flew over the Island. Most of us were outside cheering.

The Jersey Green Room Club received a notification that it was to be dissolved. We could not understand it: no reason was given. It was decided that a deputation should attend College House. The original order was amended but the various committees were obliged to be dissolved and no social activities, dances or debates could be held. However, it was finally arranged that the drama section, run by a minimum number of the committee, was allowed to function for the specific purpose for which it was created – dramatic art – and they would allow a dance to be held after each production, which had been the rule formerly.

One day my father-in-law was walking around the garden searching for a missing duck. Taking a narrow pathway he heard a noise under one of the bushes. He walked on quietly and waited a little distance away in the hope of seeing the duck emerge. When she eventually appeared he returned to the spot to discover with great glee seven eggs. This was a great find! We had been lucky enough from time to time to discover one or two eggs, but they were always found indoors before the ducks were let out in the morning. We started an intensive search for more.

The Germans exploded a mine which had been washed ashore. I was told that people in the vicinity were not warned and they were quite alarmed. Many houses were seriously damaged with roof slates and tiles blown off and windows blown out. Fortunately no-one was hurt but there were a few narrow escapes. It most likely happened soon after a naval engagement off St Malo. A British destroyer was sunk at the time and quite a number of sailors and marines were washed ashore.

A section of the Howard Davis Park was now dedicated to be used as the Island of Jersey War Cemetery for all the victims of the misfortunes of war. So of course those who had previously been buried elsewhere on the Island would be re-interred there. This lovely park would be a superb place of remembrance. Schoolchildren took it in turns to lay fresh flowers constantly on the graves.

Many people watched with great fascination from above the pier as salvage efforts were carried out in the harbour to raise a patrol boat sunk as the result of an RAF raid. Two tugs, aided by several huge army vehicles with chains attached to the submerged boat, were engaged in raising her with great difficulty. They eventually succeeded and the boat was lashed to the bollards.

Dr McKinstry, speaking to a meeting at the Brig-y-Don Children's Convalescent Home, produced some thought-provoking figures in relation to the welfare of the children. Up to the age of six the children had received sufficient food and their height and weight were normal. But for the six to ten-year-olds the rations were inadequate and badly balanced. This meant that on reaching school-leaving age, both boys and girls were on average half an inch shorter and about seven pounds lighter than they would have been outside war conditions.

These consequences would not disappear with the end of the Occupation. Tuberculosis had become rife over the whole Island, particularly bone tuberculosis, usually rare in Jersey. Also, among the population in general there had been an enormous loss of weight.

A Russian bishop and his chaplain arrived from France to consecrate a section of the 'Strangers Cemetery' where Russian slave-labourers were to be buried. Unfortunately the public were not allowed to be present, but Russian prisoners from several camps attended and were addressed by the bishop. A requiem was sung beautifully by a choir drawn from the labourers. It was all outward show as we knew only too well how badly the Germans treated their Russian prisoners-of-war.

A burial of six more British naval ratings whose bodies had been washed ashore took place at the Island War Cemetery. The Dean and Father Arscott officiated. The Bailiff and several other Island officials attended, and the Germans again supplied a guard of honour and a firing squad. Those interred there now numbered thirty-six men from the Royal Navy, two from the RAF and one US officer. This included soldiers originally buried at Mont à l'Abbé.

The fuel ration was now increased – most fortunate for the month of December – to 2 cwt of wood and 1 cwt of coal. There would also be 2oz of pipe tobacco and fifty cigarettes, 1/2 lb of margarine and a piece of toilet soap per head, 2oz of butter and 6oz of sweets for children under 18. It truly was not a great deal for one month. For Christmas the curfew hours were to be extended to midnight from the 24th to 27th and again to midnight on December 31st and January 1st.

The Jersey Green Room Club put on an excellent production of *The Merchant of Venice* at the Opera House. This production was soon followed by the annual pantomime.

The Germans celebrated their Christmas at several churches, having decorated them with Christmas trees. For us, needless to say, there was nothing to buy. A box of crackers worth 1s 6d was sold at an auction for two guineas! There were no toys for the children. It's difficult to explain the suffering of many poor families at this time.

Our Christmas was much the same as the previous year. My aunt came up with her dog and joined us for the day. I had managed to get a chicken from one of my kind farmers, but they were having trouble with many robberies committed both by locals and Germans. The latter were constantly pestering the farmers. It was difficult to hide things from them.

I'm certain that we all hoped and prayed that this was to be the last Christmas of the Occupation. How long could we go on living in such a perilous position? Mr Newland was very brave and never complained but without the medication that he required I didn't know how long he would last. He had now lost over four stone. I was still able to get brandy and we offered a toast to 1944 with the same wishes that must have been felt all over the Island. We still were able to listen to the news nearly every night. Things were good but nothing to tell us when the great day of liberation would arrive. People were still being caught for possessing wirelesses and being fined daily for unregistered livestock.

I received a Christmas card from the States Telephone Department Voluntary Relay Service expressing their thanks for assisting them in their efforts to cheer the patients and inmates of the Island institutions during the Occupation. This came as a complete surprise. I had enjoyed doing it and would continue to put on shows from time to time, taking suitable items from the performances which would be appropriate for the occasion. We also put on a concert party-type of production in between my own shows, which I took to various parish and church halls.

The sight and sound of our planes constantly attacking their targets was encouraging and cheered me up no end. It caused the Germans here much anguish. At times there was a great deal of anti-aircraft action, but the only plane that they managed to bring down was one that was already in trouble and limping home. They were becoming increasingly nervous about an invasion. Several mines were washed ashore and leaflets were dropped by the RAF written in French and dated January 20th 1944. We already knew most of this news from our wireless.

Something that I saw in the *Evening Post* which I found rather strange was that black silk stockings were available for the female population! I wonder where they had come from? I did not think that this was exactly a necessary item for a woman's wardrobe at this particular time. Surely there were many more items of clothing more urgently needed? I suppose that it was a nice gesture nonetheless.

A tremendous fire took place at A de Gruchy & Co, one of the largest shops on the Island, completely gutting a large area of the building. It was quite some time before the fire brigades from various parts of the Island arrived to help. The water supply had been turned off which did not facilitate matters. Flames could be seen from all over the Island. The restaurant, bakehouse, library, and china and rug shops were all destroyed. At that time the restaurant was being used by the Germans and they had been seen in there shortly before the fire broke out! The Germans must have lost quite a quantity of goods which had been stored there.

It was rather amusing to see some of the German officers riding around on cycles, all of which had been acquired by fair means or foul. I expect that most of the cars which they obtained locally had all gone to France or wherever. Their two horse carts trundled along the country roads driven by weary-looking soldiers. Apart from cars and lorries, furniture stored in various depositories was also being requisitioned, apparently to send over to France.

British planes passed over La Rocque and were fired on by patrol boats. One of our planes swooping down raked the boats with cannon fire. It set one on fire, which eventually blew up, while the other boat managed to limp back into St Helier Harbour. There were German casualties and I heard that a number had been killed. I would have jumped for joy if I had been able to watch the destruction.

Engine trouble had forced down an American fighter at St Peter's, severely damaged. The pilot, who had bailed out, was taken prisoner and transferred to a German hospital at the Merton Hotel before being sent to a prisoner-of-war camp in France. Apparently he had told the farmer who was first on the scene that the 'Big Show' would soon be starting, and that was great news.

Soon after this we saw hundreds of planes heading for the French coast and you could hear the bombing and feel the vibration which went on for a considerable time. We were all beginning to feel restless with high hopes and anticipation. Would the British forces soon be landing in France and if so, what would happen here?

During firing practice at the south-east corner of the Island, a considerable amount of damage was being done around Gorey village, mostly to windows. We were very worried about this as my aunt lived on the outskirts of the village; it was all very upsetting for her.

News of a lesser kind, but still most welcome, was that the next month we would have a tin of haricots verts and five cream chocolate bars (approx 4 ozs) and children would get two 8 oz packets of sweets. It was a pity that we did not receive that extra each month.

Generally, however, life was getting more difficult for everyone. It was particularly severe in the nursing homes and the Dispensary (maternity hospital), where they were obliged to manage with a meagre supply of candles.

Doctors were experiencing problems owing to the shortage of petrol. They were obliged to share cars, which was no help at all. The hospital had to be closed at one point as there was a Scarlet Fever epidemic there. Great care would have to be taken to prevent its spread throughout the Island.

Following a meeting of medical practitioners an appeal was made to the Germans for a ship to be sent to Cherbourg to procure much-needed supplies. The shortage, especially of anaesthetics, was now acute. Originally persons under two years and over eighty had been granted special licences which would give them priority in receiving whatever medical supplies were available. The Germans did suggest that they might allow the very elderly and the most serious medical cases to use their electric fires, when and if electric power was functioning.

It was cold in February with falls of snow. The lack of hot food was telling for many. There were several good benevolent charities in existence, and the children's Benefit Fund did excellent work in purchasing rations for those who were unable to afford them. The States too were helping with special child allowances for a great many. Also there were children with inadequate clothing, which was a piteous sight.

But somehow, in spite of all this, the spirit of the people was quite remarkable. I think that the constant bombing of the French coast was responsible for many cheerful faces. The thought was that perhaps the spring would bring our release: that word was imprinted on our minds.

A number of Red Cross parcels were received from Germany from friends in German internment camps, who had been able to send to relatives as they had more food than they required. Quite astonishing.

We learned that the Feld Kommandant and many of his staff were to leave the Island to make their headquarters at St Lo, administering the Island from France. The Kommandant here would now be K.V.R. von Aufsess.

Meanwhile my theatre school carried on with a great deal of improvement in the work of many pupils. Rehearsals had been in progress for *Happy Hours*, which was to be the next revue. I had hopes that it would be the final one. Special items including some costumes had been kept for that production, which would now have to go into mothballs until the great day arrived. This left me with an uneasy feeling that it was going to be difficult to keep up the high standard which I had set myself. It was so very difficult to find items worthy of presentation. Quite a lot of music had to be transcribed from my library of records, which entailed a great deal of work for my very helpful musicians.

I decided not to have any of the youngsters in this production. They were all too young and there were also too many of them for seven performances. But much to their parents' delight I decided to put on a matinee especially for them at a later date. We finally opened our *Happy Hours* revue on March 27th, which was again well received. It had been a difficult time as a bout of influenza caused some cast changes, so the eager understudies for once had their opportunity.

The Germans started visiting schools to assess the standard of teaching. They suggested more classes and at the same time obtained the names of students who had left school. The pressure appeared to be on to find people for interpreting. I somehow didn't think that they would have much luck.

It was a good thing that they never discovered that Mrs Newland spoke German – and this she had learned at her father's knee! He was the second son of the Duke of Mecklenburg Schwerin, who disinherited his son on marrying an English woman. He had been interned by the British during the 1914–1918 War and, ironically, we now saw the situation reversed. Irene was very fond of this grandfather. She had many tales to relate of the pleasureable times she spent with him when she was a little girl.

One night we listened to Mr Churchill reviewing the war situation on the wireless. As always there were no frills in his down-to-earth statements. I gather that many shorthand copies were made and distributed. In the morning we heard that Bristol had been bombed – not so good.

During the night the streets of the town had been littered with pamphlets entitled 'We Protest'. Some were even pushed through letterboxes and printed in the most obscene language. They contained pictures and cuttings mainly

Joan Gray and John Le Sueur

from American sources, and also extracts of speeches made by Allied politicians saying what a powerful enemy Germany was. If this was meant to be propaganda it was not very impressive; in fact I called it a complete disaster.

A very sad piece of news was recorded. A little boy named 'Wood' was shot by his brother with a German revolver which he must have found when out playing. At the inquest the verdict was recorded of simple accidental death.

The Germans in their excitement shot down one of their own planes which crashed down near Eden Chapel in an open field. Needless to say there were no survivors. Many people visited the wreckage and, in spite of the presence of a guard, were able to collect souvenirs.

All over the Island large pylons were being erected utilising lengths of railway line. They were sunk quite deep into the ground, irrespective of any crops being grown there, in order to prevent planes from landing. What with the pylons, railways and gun emplacements etc, the Island was becoming a scrapheap. They were highly irksome and I hoped that when the war was over the Germans would be forced to remove all this disfiguring rubbish and everything else that they had inflicted upon us. I just wondered how many houses they had pulled down or destroyed. Would we ever know?

The Germans sentenced a well-known farmer to ten months' imprisonment for being in possession of German brandy. The joke was that the sentence was to be deferred until the Germans had won the war! That wouldn't worry the farmer too much. In any case brandy was available from time to time on the black market.

In order to keep up the morale of the troops, another large-scale manoeuvre was held during the early hours. People were woken by the sound of heavy guns firing away – what a tremendous waste of ammunition! The troops trampled over gardens and fields of crops, damaging fences and everything else in their path. They also laid mines in the fields at Archirondel and, later in the morning, people in one district were even obliged to vacate their homes because of 'sharpshooting'. One person was hit by a shell splinter and had to go to hospital. This was something we had to accept under an Army of Occupation.

From time to time we were literally showered with leaflets dropped by Allied planes. On one occasion hundreds were picked up in the St Saviour area. Printed in French, they were no doubt dropped by the Americans in a raid over the French coast. The soldiers were rushed out to collect them, thereby depriving us of what might have been interesting reading matter.

Mrs Doris Stevenson produced *A Little Bit of Fluff* by Walter Ellis at Grouville Parish Hall. It was a most amusing play in which I had undertaken to play the leading male role. It was great to be working in a straight play once again, especially with a lady who had originally toured with her own professional repertory company.

The Germans were transferring large numbers of troops over to France, leaving only about 5,000 on the Island – fewer mouths to feed! Quite a number of properties which had now been reclaimed had suffered wanton damage. Friends of ours who had been obliged to vacate their large home returned to find overwhelming destruction. The lovely mahogany balustrade in the main hall had been ripped out and burnt. Unbelievable damage was found throughout the rest of the building. It was out of the question for them to return to the house in its dreadful condition.

But they were not the only ones to go through this devastating experience. Other friends on entering their house had found that the eyes had been shot out of all their portrait paintings. Two of them in particular were of immense value. It was impossible to comprehend their dismay at the sight of this dastardly act of mutilation.

We had no issue of fuel for April except by special permit on medical grounds, and the electricity ration was cut to 3 1/2 units per household. Gas was now down to 6½ hours per day: 6.30am to 8.30am, 11am to 1pm and 6.30pm to 7.30pm. It was very weak indeed.

More Red Cross letters arrived, unfortunately none for us. What was of immediate interest was the announcement on the BBC that supplies of vitamin D were being dispatched for the children of the Channel Islands and this should be sufficient for six months.

We learned that a large German ship loaded with cars from Jersey was beached at Dinard, having been damaged by Allied planes. Our planes rattled the windows once more: large squadrons of planes crossed the Island on their way to bomb more targets in northern France – a nice way of celebrating Hitler's birthday (April 20th).

There was also a mutiny of German soldiers at Portelet. I have no idea how many were implicated as this kind of news always tends to be rather dubious. However, quite a large contingent were seen being taken to Fort Regent. The place must be filled to capacity – soldiers and prisoners were constantly being incarcerated in that old fort. No doubt they would be shunted on again.

Bales of hay were washed ashore from a wreck. A local pilot based in St Helier declared that bad navigation was undoubtedly to blame. Apparently the crew had panicked. There was a large quantity of black market goods on board, but an attempt to rescue this failed.

I had my own little bit of dangerous excitement. One evening I was returning home from a late class on my old boneshaker, needless to say without a light (not the first time by any means). I reached Houge Bie. The next big house I had to pass had been converted into a military post where large numbers of soldiers were stationed. Knowing my way very well I was travelling at a fair speed and there was just sufficient light for me to spot a German sentry on duty in the centre of the road. This was unusual as normally surveillance was maintained from the entrance of the driveway.

He had his back to me. Instantly I saw my chance. I knew it was a risk but surprise would be on my side. I rode as hard as I could straight into him, sending him and his rifle flying. Loud obscene shouts followed, but I was on my way. After a moment or two shots were fired and there was more yelling, followed soon after by the sound of cars revving up furiously at the house. I hurtled down the road and around the first corner. Moments later I had dragged my cycle over the hedge into the nearest field which kept me sufficiently hidden from view. It was only a minute or two before three cars came streaming past down the main road. None turned in my direction, thank goodness.

I waited no longer as they would be back searching the side roads. I hurried on always listening and selecting my return route carefully. It took me some time to reach home, well after curfew. I felt quite pleased with myself. I had not killed a German but this was the next best thing that I could do. I don't think that the family approved, but I was happy.

The next morning I found a small piece of the guard's uniform caught in the pedal of the cycle. I would like to have kept it for my scrapbook as a souvenir, my one successful bout with the enemy. However, I felt that I should burn it in case the house was searched at any future time. As far as we knew, the Germans did not investigate this escapade any further.

On Easter Saturday 1944 lettuce and cabbage arrived from Guernsey. At other times different vegetables were exchanged between the Islands. Although some green vegs were now available, potatoes were still obtained 'under the counter'. Other than that the shops were mostly empty, with the exception of flower shops which did a roaring trade over the Easter weekend.

Someone had managed to keep a 2s Easter egg, which they were offering through the *Evening Post* to the highest bidder in aid of the Children's Benefit Fund – a nice gesture. I wondered how they had managed to keep it all that time. It finally sold for £10 13s 6d.

The following month our total weekly ration, if you can believe it, was further reduced to: 4½ lb bread, 5lb potatoes, 4oz butter, 3oz sugar, 1oz salt and 7oz breakfast meal (which was only good for the ducks). The milk ration remained at half a pint. All too frequently there was a meatless week. Owing to fluctuating circumstances goods could no longer be guaranteed during the coming months. Nothing unusual about that.

Guernsey appeared to be worse off than us. The Germans now demanded that farmers in Jersey supply one hundred head of cattle from each parish, as well as a quantity of potatoes. It was hardly surprising that they had difficulty in meeting this demand. More than likely it would go to feed the Guernsey troops, not the residents. This order certainly had not been countersigned by the Bailiff.

We heard that a soldier who had shot a German officer at La Rocque some time ago had faced the firing squad and was buried in the 'Strangers' Cemetery', which was normally kept shut at night. On arriving early, the escort party smashed the gate locks to enter. We found this a somewhat wanton piece of destruction.

There was drama on the St Helier Weighbridge when ratings started shooting at their own officers. The area was sealed off immediately. One of the sailors was taken into the JMT Garage, put against the wall and shot. It was now the turn of the Germans to live dangerously.

A deserter was also shot. The girlfriend who had been sheltering him had her death sentence commuted to ten years' imprisonment. She was from Guernsey, and surprisingly both she and her mother were allowed to attend the funeral.

We discovered that the brains behind the project at St Lawrence with its enormous workface was Dr Fritz Todt. On various occasions we had heard of Todt workers without realising that they had been involved with the vast underground construction. Many more Russians had been brought over to add to the already huge force working on the job. The poor men were treated as slaves and worked long hours in the most terrible conditions: this resulted in many accidents and deaths. Explosions were constantly heard in the neighbourhood.

Originally we had understood that artillery barracks and a stores depot were to be located there, but we later learned that it was to become a military hospital, complete with a sophisticated operating theatre.

The Germans were now becoming stricter than ever. Anyone caught outside after curfew was to be kept in a German billet overnight and then taken to College House to pay a fine. Cyclists riding two abreast were apprehended and given a stern warning, and many had their cycle numbers noted. The Germans again started checking on motor cars that might have escaped the attention of the Purchasing Commission. I just hoped they wouldn't find mine, but even if they did, they would never find the wheels!

The following story was passed on to me by someone who knew the lady involved, a resident of St Ouens. This lady bravely gave refuge to a young Russian for two years by pretending that he was her son. He even accompanied her into town and elsewhere. 'Mother and son' got wind that the Germans were onto the ruse, so the Russian again skilfully 'disappeared'. When the Germans came to the house, all they could find was one secreted wireless. She was certainly in trouble because of the wireless, but this was a much lesser offence.

We also heard of a St Martin resident who was imprisoned for giving refuge to a Russian, and there were others, some lucky, others unlucky.

It was now the month of May and my yearning to get away was increasing daily. Thoughts of my favourite canoe still hidden in the hayloft beckoned me, but I tried hard to keep it out of my mind as I knew that it was quite impossible for me to desert the family at such a time. Nonetheless, those thoughts continued to rear their ugly heads from time to time. Just how long would I have to keep this up? I wished that I could see the writing on the wall.

There was a terrific explosion one night. An ammunition ship had been bombed by the Allies somewhere off the French coast. The Germans were extremely disturbed and apparently expected something to happen here very soon. They again started hectic operations with intensive gunfire. Some people were greatly alarmed at being obliged to vacate their homes for several hours. A terrific amount of damage was done to fences and gardens, and growing crops were utterly disregarded. After that more and more people were turned out of their homes and more land mines were laid.

We heard that German soldiers were trying to buy lead and iron, which was very strange as they had quantities of railway lines stored in dumps all over the Island. I suspected that 'A' was not aware of what 'B' was doing. Perhaps this would be remedied by the arrival of our latest Kommandant, Colonel Heine. He auspiciously styled himself 'Kommandant of the Fortress of Jersey'.

The power station built by the Germans in St Peter's Valley was operating only occasionally though most of the coal available on the Island had been requisitioned to keep it working. It was widely believed that the plant was proving to be unsatisfactory because the French engineers who built it had perpetrated a little sabotage during the construction.

On June 4th Mr A Harrison, a well-liked old Victorian who had been the co-proprietor and managing director of the *Evening Post* for many years, died. He would be sorely missed.

CHAPTER EIGHT

WINGS OVER JERSEY

Listening to the BBC on the evening of June 4th we heard the astonishing news that Rome had fallen! This was stupendous. Surely this called for a drink, but could we spare it? Mrs Newland quickly nodded her agreement. The following night we were even more ecstatic. We were awakened by the increasing sound of wave after wave of planes flying overhead and we at once realised that this, at last, must be the invasion of France. Joy knew no bounds and I almost fell out of bed with excitement.

The Germans here put up a terrific barrage which continued constantly through the night, creating horrendous reverberation. As soon as there was a glimmer of daylight we were up to observe everything. There were planes of every description flying overhead. On the ground all was chaos. Ambulances were rushing all over the place. Panic reigned supreme among our disorganised German oppressors, and it was laughable to see these poor wretched soldiers running around wearing Red Cross armlets, thinking that this gave them added protection in spite of already being fully equipped with helmets and rifles. They risked deep trouble as this was in utter defiance of the Geneva Convention.

After all this wild excitement we decided we simply must retreat indoors to have some very late breakfast. Of course this had to be preceded by downing a brandy and toasting success to all Allied troops involved in the gigantic operation on which they were embarking. Mrs Newland suggested that we should open a tin of sardines for dinner that night by way of celebration.

Red Cross flags swiftly made their appearance on many buildings, even those where large numbers of the German Army were billeted. The garrison was now down to 7,000 but there still appeared to be masses of guards all over the place. The Secret Police had now donned their uniforms, and guards were stationed at the gasworks and electricity station. The telephone service had been taken over, but this did not worry us for we all knew what was happening. About a hundred Frenchmen who had been working for the Germans took advantage of this situation and did not turn up for work. They were unlucky as they were soon rounded up and taken to Fort Regent.

A surprising item of news came to us through the BBC which is worth mentioning. It was announced that there had been an attack on the Channel Islands – and that the wireless station at Fort George in Guernsey had been bombed for the second time. I could see that our Allied airmen might occasionally attack some of the isolated German gun positions on the Islands, just to keep them in suspense.

The following notice then appeared:

'To the population of the States of Jersey

Germany's enemy is on the point of attacking French soil. I expect the population of Jersey to keep its head, to remain calm, and to refrain from any acts of sabotage and from hostile acts against German forces, even should the fighting spread to Jersey. At the first signs of unrest or trouble, I will close the streets to all traffic and will secure hostages. Attacks against the German Forces will be punished by death.

Kommandant der Festung, Jersey

signed Heine, Jersey 6th June 1944

The next day I went to the studio as usual and to my surprise nearly everyone was there. All were very excited and anxious to know what I was going to do about our Liberation production. I must admit that I was rather unprepared for such eagerness. Naturally I did have some definite new ideas to be added to my original plans for the final show. I must say that classes that day and the rest of the week were rather wild; concentration simply did not exist, but it was excusable. I would have to get busy as there was no knowing when that final production would be. The pressure was on.

The BBC announced that a small successful raid had been made on Sark in order to ascertain whether any farmers had been deported to Germany. The desired information had been obtained with all the correct details. They also announced that a German convoy between Guernsey and Cap de la Hague had been intercepted by British boats and that an ammunition ship had been blown up. All this was such good news. How lucky we were to have our wireless set; it helped to keep us going.

A Frenchman whose plane was damaged while over Guernsey and unable to get back to base landed in Trinity. He destroyed much of the plane's mechanism to prevent the enemy from making use of it. Before the Germans arrived to take him to prison he had a good chat with the locals, and was able to give them the welcome news that everything was going well in England and that the collapse of Italy could happen at any time.

The anti-aircraft guns had opened fire and a German shell had fallen in a garden quite close to our friends at Bagatelle, St Saviour. No German planes were seen these days. Ammunition from Fort Regent was now being transferred to the tunnel which the Germans had dug at the Grand Vaux valley. They still continued to erect gunposts in the eastern parishes because of their proximity to the French coast. My aunt said that they were requisitioning gardens in Gorey for that very purpose, much to local people's annoyance.

Preparation to defend the Island was now obvious. Troops had been taken out of town to be billeted in the homes of people in various parts of the country. More and more gunposts were appearing around the Island, but several of them were machine-gunned by Allied planes en route to France. We could hear the sound of bombing from the direction of Carteret, the nearest small French port to Jersey. We were very much aware that it was now the turn of the poor citizens of this town to be caught up in the terrible fighting.

We were delighted to hear Harry Le Sueur, the American NBC war correspondent, report that he could actually see Jersey and more importantly that some British troops who had originally come from the Island had been found and released. Great news. We wondered if, with a name like his, he was actually a Jerseyman.

The carelessness of the Germans was once more exhibited when they took the Jersey lifeboat Howard I from its shed to launch it. They lost control and it swerved into a wall, seriously damaging its bow. So now, until repairs could be completed, we were deprived of the most valuable sea service.

Five young men attempted a carefully-planned escape from Fauvic, carrying letters of introduction to Jerseymen in England. Various people saw them off and helped lift their boats over the sea wall. They had hoped to arrange to have a signal beamed from Portbail Lighthouse on the French coast to signify their safe arrival. The signal was duly beamed. Unfortunately another four who made an escape attempt from the same beach were dashed against the rocks and drowned.

Meanwhile the BBC announced that an area off the French coast including the Channel Islands was unsafe for fishermen as a free-bombing policy was coming into force with immediate effect. This might curtail our friends' movements, I thought.

One evening we learned that the major French towns of Rennes and Dinan had fallen to the Allies. It was encouraging to hear that we were making swift progress down the coast. Big boats docked in the harbour were departing for Brest and I could see that our communications with France were practically at an end. Unless the Germans moved out now they would be trapped with us until the end of the war. Oh horror!

Several days later the BBC announced that St Malo was now in the hands of the Allies. St Helier Harbour, including the small boat anchorages, was now crowded with vessels of every category. Most of them came from ports along the

French coast bringing large numbers of soldiers and sailors – about 2,000 in all. They crowded into the town and its pubs. Some of the French would be more than happy to find work on the farms here just for food without pay.

The activity along the French coast was tremendous and we wondered about the fate of the people there. More great news was that Cherbourg had been captured by the Allies. But unfortunately all the news was not good news. We heard that an escort of ships had arrived here from Guernsey. It being low tide they were seen landing in the mud, up to 1,500 people in all. Most of them were French prisoners who had been forced to work in Guernsey. They were immediately taken to Fort Regent where they remained until weather conditions improved sufficiently for them to continue their journey to France. Also on board were a few Jerseymen who had been drafted to work on Alderney. They related many tales about life in the concentration camps on our small sister island.

We Islanders felt intense indignation that fifteen civilians who had been sentenced to two months' imprisonment or more for various political reasons were now being taken to France. People gathered near the harbour to see them off. Many 'V' signs were in evidence. We learned later that their destination was a German concentration camp. Sad to say, many of them never returned. It was quite unbelievable that human beings could be subjected to such treatment for so small an offence.

Heavy bombing continued day after day and we felt the vibrations. The Americans now occupied Granville and Aramanches.

To our joy the BBC announced that the German convoy off St Malo had been intercepted by British naval forces. Two heavily-armed trawlers were sunk and others damaged. Later the body of a high-ranking German military officer wearing his Iron Cross decoration was picked up by a local fisherman at Corbiere. The body appeared not to have been in the water very long.

Also on the BBC came helpful instructions in how to make crystal sets. We did not require one just now, but later we most certainly would if we were no longer able to get our battery charged (on the quiet). I felt certain, however, that many people would be happy to take advantage of this useful information.

The Germans issued the following notice in an attempt to undermine our morale:

PROCLAMATION

'Whenever German forces have occupied territory they have safeguarded the supplies of foodstuffs and essential commodities for the civilian population. To this the British Channel Islands have been no exception.

'The British Command, on the other hand, does its worst to hamper and interrupt the steady flow of supplies to the Islands, regardless of the fact that the population of the Islands are their own fellow countrymen. Since as a result of these 'nuisance raids' the rations of the civil population have to be reduced, they may thank their countrymen across the Channel for such measures.

'Mr Churchill and the men behind him will not achieve any military results with their nuisance raids. But it is typical of their well-known ruthlessness and lack of consideration that they do not refrain from exposing their own countrymen to hardships and sufferings which might well be avoided. At least, however, the Island population ought to know the guilty party!'

Der Oberbefehlshaber der Armee

Details of arrangements for communal cooking were distributed. This was to cover the cessation of gas and electricity current as well as fuel for Aga cookers. Oven space was being allocated at various bakehouses; a charge of 3d per container was to be levied. In addition if you wished to avail yourself of the communal restaurant you would be obliged to use meat and potato ration coupons. This Irene and I did on one or two occasions so that we could join up with friends whom we seldom saw.

The Royal Jersey Agricultural and Horticultural Society held a meeting with the Farmers Union to discuss the latest German demands. Out of twelve tons of butter still in store, the Germans had had the audacity to demand eight tons. Production at this time of year was down to only twenty-five hundredweight per week. As our 2oz weekly rations required about forty-eight hundredweight it was impossible to meet the target. We did not know what butter ration the forces actually received.

Another demand called for further milch-cows to be slaughtered for meat, and this meant that even less milk would be available. The shortage of food was being keenly felt by almost everyone, and when the Germans suggested that the civilian population should only have skimmed milk, everyone was most upset. Fortunately this plan was shelved, at least for the time being.

There were some unrealistic people who, simply out of selfishness, amassed and hoarded large amounts of food which they acquired through their wealth and black market transactions. Consequently they had been able to continue enjoying a more or less normal diet, while others could hardly eke out an existence. We felt that such a selfish attitude ought to be punished by confiscation of their cache. In Germany during the 1914–18 War 'hoarders' who acted against the interests of the general community were imprisoned with hard labour and even suffered the death penalty.

The Germans began boasting that they had every intention of staying here until the end of the war. They were likely to hold out as long as they continued requisitioning our foodstuffs. We would soon be in a sorry state if fresh supplies didn't arrive. The farmers had been warned of this and so were busy hiding stocks.

Since adequate milk supplies for the Island were not forthcoming, new instructions were issued which contained very bad news for the farming community. Six farmers had their herds confiscated for not reaching the required level of production. This would also have serious repercussions for us. Juveniles over fifteen would receive the same as adults – half a pint on four days of the week – but there would be no extra milk for schoolchildren nor for invalids over sixty-five.

The German garrison was also affected. Its quota was reduced from ten thousand pots to nine thousand pots. The situation was going from bad to worse.

Our friends who lived near Bel Royal told us that several 5.9mm guns were being erected in their vicinity. I must say that our tyrants continued to be persistent in their endeavour to fortify the Island, although in my opinion it was an altogether quite useless strategy. It would just be another target for the Allies, that is, as long as the placements were not too close to local homes. Billets for gun crews were being sought in these areas. Residents would not find this a happy situation.

A hospital ship arrived with between two and three hundred wounded. This would give the German doctors plenty of work. Quite a number of Americans were also on board and were now in hospital. One could see them waving from the windows. For these men the sudden change from wholesome US rations to the prison junk served here was quite horrific. They found it absolutely repugnant and named the so-called soup 'Nazi hog-swill'. This assessment was something I could fully endorse from my own experience. We later heard that three of their number died and were buried in the Howard Davis Park Cemetery.

The *Evening Post* published the following statement: 'The Superior Council of the States has resolved with the Occupying Forces that a supply of iron rations should be kept as an emergency for use during any period when food might not be available. Each person will receive 3lb of bread, 5lb of potatoes, 3oz of sugar, 2oz of butter, 8oz of macaroni and one tin of sardines. Children born after July 1st will receive twelve tins of condensed milk. This must not be consumed but kept for emergency. Anything perishable should be replaced from the normal ration. Kindling wood also comes under this emergency plan.'

An Allied seaplane apparently came down in St Ouen's Bay. It had picked up survivors from a naval engagement not too far away. A gunpost opened fire as the plane took off with its heavy load but with their usual accuracy the Germans failed to score a hit (most likely because they were either drunk or bewildered).

On the other hand, the German officer who shot down an American plane was reduced in rank. I wondered why the Germans had all those gunposts if they didn't want results. The seven Americans from that disaster, whose bodies had been washed up on shore, were buried in the war cemetery.

As time went on the German officials became more and more unscrupulous, commandeering horses for making sausagemeat. They required three hundred and fifty horses and only offered about twenty pounds each. This proved to be unsatisfactory as who would want to surrender their horses, never mind for such a paltry sum!

The soldiers themselves were disgruntled. They said that all they got to eat was potato soup. Sailors were now being trained to become part of the Army of Defence. There were estimated to be over 14,000 men on the Island, of which 650 were seriously wounded. There was a serious lack of medication and a Jersey doctor had at last been accepted by German staff to help out in these circumstances. The hospital was now in an abominable condition.

When I visited the Payns they had a couple of interesting stories to tell. The first, which I found quite extraordinary, took place in June 1944 and concerned a group of four soldiers at Seymour Tower, off the south-east coast of the Island. The Germans had not fully occupied the tower but went there fairly often.

On this occasion, the four men did not appear to realise how swiftly the tide could rise, and became stranded on a rock. From the shore they were watched by members of their own forces, who made no effort to go to their rescue. There was a boat available but the Germans on shore declined to use it and forbade the locals to either. They just stood watching as the four stood close together while the tide crept up. They kept their rifles above their heads and as the water reached their necks they fired their last shots before the sea closed over them.

The next day they were discovered, dead, still upright against the rock, still in line and belted together. I wondered whether they had had a pact to end their lives in this way. It seemed inconceivable that they should be left to drown in that fashion when they could easily have been rescued.

The second story which the Payns told me was also remarkable. A French boy, Roger Le Renouille, was at that time working for the Germans at the harbour in order to collect as much information as he could about gun emplacements etc which he then intended to take back to France.

He and Basil Le Brun had made friends with Bertram Payn whom they persuaded to assist them in their escape from the Island, along with three others. They wanted Bertram to help transport a boat which they had stolen from the harbour and hidden in a store on the pier. They managed to move it safely in a horse-drawn van, camouflaged by potato barrels and a tarpaulin, to a deserted shed behind a house at La Rocque, where it would be painted and prepared for the crossing by willing helpers.

Bertram selected a suitable place along the coast at Fauvic and, when the day for the escape arrived, he again helped to transport the boat in his van. They took a route along lanes where it was unlikely that they would meet any troops but, rounding a bend, they were horrified to see two German soldiers coming towards them, one on either side of the road. There was nothing that they could do but drive on, looking straight ahead as if they were on normal business, although Bertram knew that the boat was only partly covered and that some of it protruded out of the back of the van. Luckily the Germans took no notice, and the transportation party arrived safely at their destination. They unloaded the boat, concealed it and returned to the house for a brief farewell party.

So on September 4th the four were seen off after dark. Unfortunately the engine they had hoped to use was too powerful for the little boat and they had to dump it and row all the way. Nevertheless, five hours later, they reached the coast of France.

German patrols were becoming increasingly active along the coast, as a result of these escape attempts. We heard that a party of eight got away from St Aubin's Bay and two more from Le Hocq. I gather that they were all successful. But unfortunately the three who left from Fauvic were fired on by the Germans and were obliged to come ashore at Gorey.

The Germans published a notice warning that 'desertion to the enemies of the German forces' was forbidden and would be severely punished as espionage. Furthermore, in future these deserters could no longer count on being rescued by the German forces. We had heard that some deserters had got away at various times, one with some local people. But there were many goings-on that we didn't know about.

It was announced through the BBC that a question had been raised in the House of Commons with regard to the possible surrender of the Channel Islands, but that the Germans had refused. It was also reported that there was no knowledge of any ill-treatment of the civilian population on the Islands.

The gas supply was now completely terminated and the amount of electricity severely reduced. Obtaining wood had been difficult for some time, but I still hoped to be able to get some as before for a little while longer. However, we had further inspiring news: Paris was liberated! This called for another swig of brandy. I wondered what Hitler's reaction would be.

Time was marching on and the date for my children's promised production was at hand. On their great day everything went according to plan. I was agreeably surprised in the way the children concentrated so well on their various ensembles and little parts. I felt truly proud of them and they performed extremely well. The house was filled with adoring parents and their friends, who all appeared to be delighted. I appreciated the help of some of the older girls and the sterling work of Miss Maude Glendewar – in full charge of the orchestra – and of Madame Blondeau, who took such great trouble with the costumes. I just didn't know what I would have done without their help. Altogether it was a most happy and successful matinee.

I must say that I was immensely glad to have this one under my belt so that I could now devote myself to working towards a top-flight Liberation production. The question was, when would we be liberated?

From time to time reductions to the bus timetable had been made, but in November we were notified that the service would be terminated on December 30th. The last few weeks had been pretty hopeless anyway. Some people had not been able to get into town for months, and unless you had a cycle – with tyres – or you could walk the distance, you were marooned.

Neither Irene nor I had cycle lights, which made it almost impossible to see, so I would sing all the way home with Irene following close behind me. You may well guess what the songs were. 'There'll always be an England' was one of our favourites!

Irene did not attend many classes, only rehearsals when needed. She, I feared, was feeling the lack of good food and consequently was tired out after the cycle ride home following a strenuous class. However, I had managed to obtain late-night permits for us both some time ago, so it was not quite so much of a rush.

Some short items of interest:

1. French workers imprisoned at Fort Regent were seen making their escape down the walls.

2. Soldiers who visited barbers' shops kept their rifles between their knees while being shaved.

3. Latest articles on sale from France were a large number of ladies' and gents' umbrellas!

4. Many of the Islanders being held in prison had furniture sent in to make themselves more at home (certainly different to the severity we encountered!).

5. American prisoners of war on the Island collected over £50 which they intended to divide amongst local charities. This was a mark of appreciation for the Thanksgiving Dinner which had been sent to them by some kindly local residents.

Deputy Edward Le Quesne, head of the Jersey Department of Labour, was sentenced to seven months' imprisonment for possessing a wireless, but he was allowed out one day a week to attend to business. It was later learned that if he behaved himself, he would only do two weeks now and the rest after the war!

All Islanders who had been to prison, including me, were facetiously called 'Old Gloucestonians' (the prison being in Gloucester Street). Detective Constable Shenton also joined the club, being sentenced to four months for having a wireless, and additional time for daring to retain his camera. I hoped that he had some good photos secreted away. And so it went on. People were no longer being careful because there were too many people being sentenced to prison. It was therefore a case of a quick in and out.Great excitement swept the Island at a statement made in the House of Commons that supplies of food, medicine and soap were to be shipped to the people of the Channel Islands. Later we heard that the British Government had even been approached by the German government to send further supplies to the Channel Islands. In view of reports received regarding conditions on the Islands, the British Government granted the request to dispatch food parcels similar to those sent to prisoners of war.

The following announcement was made in the *Evening Post* and signed by the Bailiff, A.M. Coutanche:

> 'A Swedish ship will be sailing next week from Lisbon and it is hoped that a representative of the International Red Cross will also be on board to investigate the actual situation of the Channel Islands and hopefully arrange for further supplies. The Department of Transport is now asking for the names of farmers who can help with horse and van to assist in the transport of the Red Cross parcels when they arrive.'

We heard that the Germans were at the banks once more. Gold, silver and securities belonging to French and other foreign nationals were being packed, ready to be transferred on the Germans' orders.

Meanwhile, local residents were having trouble drying their clothes – a distressing problem caused by the lack of fuel. This partly accounted for trees being felled all over the Island. The hillsides were being stripped and the whole Island now looked disfigured. People had removed their wooden gates some time ago as anything wooden would otherwise be stolen. It would take a long time before the Island's natural beauty was restored.

I could now report a pig case. A breeder was fined the largest amount of the war so far, £450 plus £25 costs, for having slaughtered one of his pigs. Many such instances were appearing in the local paper nearly every week. Probably over one hundred farmers and others had been caught in similar circumstances, and this would continue as people were so desperate for food.

In the meantime the bakers' ovens were working quite successfully for people without sufficient fuel for cooking to take a pan or saucepan daily to be cooked. My aunt availed herself of this provision in Gorey fairly often.

Unfortunately it was rather far for us, especially as the saucepan had to be taken down, and then another journey made later to fetch it back. Two journeys both there and back were not possible for the older folk under the present conditions. In any case, any food needed to be eaten hot would have to be rewarmed when we got back to the house. But it was a great asset if you lived near the baker.

It was good too for people who lived near the Ann Street Brewery in St Helier as they could obtain hot water free of charge. It would have been nice if hot showers could also have been installed, but sadly this was just a pipedream on our part.

The Department of Agriculture was now about to make our poor horses suffer as their owners had to donate half the yearly ration of oats which meant about 7½ cwt. This was intended to be used for the manufacture of breakfast food. If it turned out to be anything like what was served to me in prison it should be kept for the horses, I thought.

We now believed that some unauthorised German units were visiting homes on the excuse of searching for wireless sets, but with the main object of searching the cupboards to see if there were any foodstuffs they could pillage. Also, the regular troops, while engaged in carting away blocked farm produce, had been ordered to count poultry. Was this merely a straightforward census, I asked myself. We all had doubts about the German statements. However, the BBC had just broadcast that the Channel Islands would be receiving supplies, so you can imagine how overjoyed everyone was with that welcome news. Soon afterwards we were alerted to the fact that there would most likely be Red Cross letters arriving at the same time as the food parcels, and that we could write Red Cross letters and hand them in at the Bailiff's Enquiry Office.

Foreign workers, mainly French, brought here by the Germans were most likely suffering more than anyone else. They offered any amount of money to obtain something to eat. They openly declared that they were especially short of potatoes, and very nearly starving. They of course had no chance of receiving Red Cross parcels.

Town-dwellers were now visiting the country in the hope of collecting a promised bird for Christmas. In spite of the fact that the Germans were no longer going to confiscate poultry, they now demanded that 2,000 head be delivered alive on December 22nd with each parish to supply the required quota. Hopefully they would get a selection of scraggy birds. We were cheered to learn that we would each have a small tin of tunny fish for our Christmas fare, as well as a double ration of flour. But unfortunately the latter would not be available during the following week.

As regards Christmas gifts, it was a case of giving each other something that we already had. All I could give Irene was an IOU.

We had been to see the man who had taken some pictures of us in costume from my ballet *The Knave among the Hearts* (as a professional he had managed to retain his camera) and had persuaded him to enlarge a couple of pictures. He did this well and had also found frames for them, so we were able to give one to my aunt and one to Irene's parents. In return they promised us some of their lovely china after the war. Those words 'after the war' were so very often in our minds. We knew what we wanted, but at present it was in reality a dream, an adventure into the unknown.

Mrs Newland decided that this Christmas, dinner had to be as near as possible to a normal one and so the best china, silver and glass graced the table. There were lovely flowers and crackers, which had been made out of crepe paper most imaginatively to make an attractive decoration. It all looked beautiful.

My aunt was with us again for lunch but had not brought 'Chummy', her dog. She was so afraid that even with him on the lead he could be snatched away. Quite high prices were now being offered by the Germans for cats and dogs and she had nearly lost him once before.

We were lucky that we had been able to get hold of a nice fat chicken for the five of us, with potatoes and brussel sprouts from our gardener, who had a good high-walled garden not subjected to robberies (I should think one of the few). He was a jovial old boy with quite a sense of humour: he once proudly displayed the ninth patch on his trousers, which bore a strong resemblance to a patchwork quilt. He said with some amusement that his underwear was actually made from a blanket.

We had a Christmas pudding of sorts which was barely edible but was saved by a brandy sauce. My aunt had brought a box of dates which she had hoarded for such an occasion, and we did have a good bottle of wine. She was certain that it would be our last Christmas of the war, and we had many toasts. We all prayed for the end of the Occupation and an end to all wars.

My aunt left early and so Irene and I walked her home, which was quite a distance away. Strictly speaking it was rather too much for her. Timmy insisted on coming and I felt that I would be able to manage if anyone tried to snatch him as we were all armed with stout walking sticks. It had turned out to be a lovely sunny day but rather cold. Poor little dog, he was not his usual self. Normally he would pull us along on his lead. Instead on the uphill return journey he was slow. His diet, which consisted mostly of limpets, was of no appeal. He like us was losing his strength.

The curfew over Christmas was set as follows: on December 23rd, 24th and 25th it would be until midnight, and on New Year's Eve until 12.30am.

On Boxing Day the Green Room Club presented the Christmas pantomime *Aladdin* at the Opera House. This would run until January 6th. It would most likely be the last show of the Occupation as the permanent suspension of electricity could happen any day.

The problem of fuel had become even more acute. The Department of Labour had begun felling the lovely trees in the Royal Crescent and those in other terraces of the town. Our own stocks of wood were now pretty low and it was imperative that I should try to obtain more. It was dusk when I left the house and crossed the garden to the small gate which led to the hill, sometimes used by our German intruders. I crossed the road and made my way along the driveway to the back of a farmyard. I had seen German carts loaded with wood crossing from this direction and that was what I was determined to procure. Passing along the far wall I followed the wide pathway which led across the end of a field. It was still light enough for me to see the circles of short grass where the cattle had been tethered. As I passed into the next field I could discern the wheel marks which led to trees in the distance. Following the pathway I eventually entered the wood and proceeded down a slope. I soon discovered a section where trees had been felled. Brambles and brushwood littered the space but there was no sign of any logs.

Retracing my way to the top I discovered more wheel tracks in the grass heading along the top of the wood which I at once followed. Imagine my delight when, rounding a bend, I saw a large pile of huge logs just waiting for collection. By this time darkness had caught up with me. It was difficult to find a log small enough to handle. I finally selected one of the smaller ones, about 8ft long but pretty thick. It was heavy going as I trudged along dragging my trophy. I was obliged to make occasional stops.

I had just about reached the end of the first field when I heard a dog barking, followed shortly after by the rumble of a cart. I could not for a moment imagine that they would come to collect wood at this late hour. Panic seized me – what should I do? To the right of the track there was a drop of a few feet into a field of swedes and so without hesitation and with great difficulty I dragged the log over the bank and down into the field below. This is where I lay under the bank among brambles and nettles in the long wet grass, hanging onto the end of my log.

It seemed an interminably long time before the carts and their jabbering drivers passed slowly by. I breathed a sigh of relief as they vanished down the track in the rain. Now, how was I going to get out of here? I could never get the log back up onto that pathway again, so I dragged it along the side of the bank, finally finding an opening about fifty yards on. I was worried that I wouldn't be able to get it home before the carts returned as there was still quite a way to go.

Eventually I reached the farmyard wall and began to approach the main road, which was going to be a difficult crossing. I was only twenty yards away when a car that had been stationary around the corner started off down the hill. My heart stopped and I became glued to the spot. Whew! Somewhat shaken I crossed the road and with great difficulty managed to get it up the steps into the garden. I parked it on a side path in case our friends came through.

I reached the house sopping wet, scratched and covered in mud. The first thing was a clean-up but for a moment I revelled in the triumph of having achieved my mission. Timmy would not stop barking at my appearance. They had all been very worried as I had been gone for such a long time. When I came down from the bathroom there were no lights and all were seated around the fire; potatoes were roasting in the hot ashes and we would have apples to follow. We had had the last of the soup at lunchtime and the eggs had to be kept for tomorrow. Mrs Newland was so sorry that, after I had been through this dreadful experience, she had nothing more to give me. Of course I had to relate my adventures. Once the Red Cross parcels arrived things would be easier for us, but wood would still be a very necessary requirement.

Meanwhile back at the theatre school, some of the students wanted to arrange a dance at the studio during the Christmas vacation. It was agreed that they should go ahead provided that they finished well before curfew and cleaned up afterwards. We decided rather sorrowfully that we should not be able to attend as my cycle was not going to manage many more trips and must be reserved for the important requirements. I placed a huge card in the main studio wishing them all a happy time. Classes would recommence on January 14th 1945, and every effort would be made to put on a grand celebration production.

CHAPTER NINE

AT LAST THE *VEGA*

December 30th 1944 was a Red Letter Day for Jersey. After endless waiting the longed-for Red Cross ship *Vega* arrived, flying the flag of the International Red Cross at her foremast and the Swedish flag at her stern, while her superstructure illuminated two Red Cross insignias.

It was a day that will always live in our memory. On board were members of the International Red Cross Commission, the Chief of the Red Cross at Lisbon and Colonel Isalin of the Swiss Army. A description of the arrival was broadcast from the tower at St Helier's Parish Church. The *Evening Post* later wrote that only those who had knowledge of how so many of the poorest inhabitants had lived during the past months could imagine what this day meant. Medical supplies, foodstuffs and soap that were all so urgently needed were now being provided, and a commission would be set up to decide what other supplies were required. So, ending the old year on a brighter note, we entered 1945 with the knowledge that, although hard and difficult times still had to be faced, our position was now far less serious than it might have been.

German sailors and marines worked on the unloading, and members of the St John's Ambulance Brigade were on the quay to watch over the operation, lend assistance and accompany the laden trolleys to a store on the Esplanade where they were checked and stored before being passed on to the grocers for distribution.

The route to the store was patrolled by German troops, the civil police and St John's Ambulance. The transport was undertaken by the farmer volunteers who had harnessed their horses to merchants' trolleys. The parcels were a gift from the Canadian Red Cross, each weighing approximately 9lbs 12ozs. There was also a limited number of special invalid parcels, the gift of the British Red Cross. New Zealand also sent soap, medical stores and a quantity of cigarettes and tobacco. The Lady Campbell Fund, created by the wife of the British Ambassador in Lisbon, sent a number of layettes. On board was also a large quantity of salt from Lisbon.

The excitement in the town was just tremendous. People were kissing and dancing in the streets with wild abandon. But for us in the Parish of St Martin's

January 6th was our day of excitement when we could at last collect our parcels. Irene and I fetched them on our bicycles. We could hardly wait to get them home and rip open the boxes with exclamations of delight as the various items appeared.

The parcels contained: 6oz of chocolate, 20 ship's biscuits, 4oz of tea, 20oz of butter, 6oz of sugar, 2oz tin of 'Klim' milk powder, 16oz tin of marmalade, 14oz tin of corned beef, 13oz tin of ham, 10oz tin of salmon, 5oz tin of sardines, 6oz tin of raisins, 6oz tin of prunes, 4oz tin of cheese, 3oz tablet of soap, and 1oz of pepper and salt. We each unpacked our own box, made separate piles on the table and just stood there gloating over the wonderful array.

We decided there and then that we should each take charge of our chocolate and biscuits and eat them when we so desired. The rest of the things would be taken up to the bedroom at night in case of a break-in. However, all our doors were pretty well secure; no-one could break in through the kitchen door as apart from a good lock we had a very effective booby-trap which we always set up once we were all in the house at night.

We would celebrate that evening and all were in favour of having salmon. It was impossible to know when we might receive another parcel so we would have to be very careful with this most welcome gift. Mrs Newland was already planning how she would organise some of our future meals. The unexpected addition of a tin of sardines on each of our ration books was an extra help.

The Department of Public Health informed us of the possible evacuation by the Red Cross of invalids in about three months' time. It might be to a neutral country rather than England. The hospital ship would only take about sixty patients from Jersey and they would have to travel unaccompanied.

Mr Newland would not apply: he had no intention of going by himself, particularly to an unknown country. He was determined to stay with us to the bitter end, no matter when that would be. I sincerely hoped that he would be able to last out. It would be three long months before all the negotiations between Great Britain and Germany could be concluded. Only then would the hospital ship be allowed to bring out all the eligible invalids and sick people. But it was good news for those who would be able to make the journey.

My bicycle was now a big problem. The back tyre was completely finished, having been patched up beyond all recognition. The front one would soon be in the same state. With the greatest difficulty I managed to replace it with rope, but that only lasted for about a fifteen-minute ride. I then wired a length of hosepipe in place and this was more successful. It lasted for three trips into town and several local journeys, allowing me to collect our milk and rations, before it spun off quite dangerously. The wire had evidently cut through the pipe. I was obliged to go through the same process several times before the end

Labels and packs of some of the Red Cross supplies.

of the Occupation.

Fortunately Irene's bicycle was in much better condition, and unless she was with me I used hers. If we had to go somewhere together we had a system which worked quite well. First of all, one rode on ahead but before going out of sight, left the cycle in full view of the other person, who was walking up behind. The other, on reaching the cycle, would mount and cycle up to and on past the new walker. This was quicker than walking all the way and less tiring. Of course there were some places where it was impossible to use this system, and also, it could only be employed in daylight.

The American prisoners of war, Captain Clark and Lieutenant Haas, escaped from the German prisoner of war camp. It was expressly announced that if any of the civilian population extended help and took them in they would be killed. This would also apply if they tried to assist any Russian prisoners who escaped from time to time.

The *Vega* left port on January 4th carrying the Commissioner's report on the state of the situation on the Island: this report would be presented to the British Government. The Bailiff had informed the Commission in no uncertain terms as to the Island's requirements. The Germans insisted on attending all the conferences, as they always did, but that did not prevent straight talking. The latest news of the *Vega* was that she might have to

NOTICE

On January 8th, 1945, the American prisoners - of - war Captain Clark and Lieutenant Haas escaped from the German prisoner - of - war camp. They will attempt to obtain shelter and help from the English civilian population.

It is expressly announced that anyone who takes in or extends help in any way to Captain Clark or Lieutenant Haas will be punished by death according to paragraph 9 of the Order for the Protection of the Occupying Forces.

DESCRIPTION.

Captain Clark. About 29 to 31 years old. Fair, curly hair, brushed back. Slim athletic build, about 5 ft. 8 ins. to 5 ft. 9 ins., small face, looks ill, grey eyes. Probably wearing American uniform (khaki) and fatigue dress.

Lieutenant Haas. About 22 to 24 years old. Dark hair, sticks up somewhat, small, pale, boyish face lower jaw somewhat prominent, dark eyes. Face long and full. Tall, slim build about 5ft. 9 ins. to 5 ft. 11 ins. Limps somewhat due to a wound in the leg. Probably wearing American uniform (khaki) shirt or fatigue dress.

Der Kommandant Festung Jersey

gez. HEINE

Oberst.

Jersey, 8/1/45.

undergo repairs before returning as her keel had been damaged off Guernsey. Fortunately these were completed quickly and she was able to return by the end of that month, bringing further supplies.

There would now be available household and toilet soap, candles, matches, salt and sugar. We would be glad to be able to get these items. I was especially keen on the candles as of late we had been going to bed when it got dark at five o'clock, accompanied by our evening meal, a ship's biscuit, which had arrived in our food parcel.

Not such good news was that some of the parcels had been tampered with. As many as 269 were found to be deficient and needed to be repacked. The Bailiff issued the following statement: 'I do not believe that any person in any way connected with the handling of the cargo in Jersey waters or on Jersey soil is responsible for the deficiencies.' Later a youth was given eighteen strokes of the birch for having stolen a parcel.

The Germans were again obliged to annex another hotel for their prisoners. I thought that they must have more than they could cope with. Robberies continued unabated, as did searches carried out by the Germans for food, cattle, pigs and wireless sets. The overall lack of food was resulting in a breakdown of law and order, in spite of the imposition of heavy fines and the increasing number of arrests. Thoughts of liberation took a back seat, for what our minds and bodies desired more than anything else was food and warmth.

Here we were starting 1945. It should have been full of hope and expectations, but I felt terribly depressed. Everyone had lost weight. Mr Newland was now down to eight stone from fourteen stone. Irene lacked her normal energy. Mrs Newland would not give us her weight, but we could tell that she was down. She did her best with the little food she had at her disposal. She was very worried about her husband. So many people around the Island looked poorly and despondent.

During January we were warned that the electricity supply would be stopped. Owing to circumstances beyond the authorities' control, they were no longer able to continue even the limited supply available during the previous four months. This would be devastating for everyone, particularly during these winter months. We only had a few candles which we were keeping for an emergency. I was told that you could buy them on the black market for £1 each. It was dark by five o'clock, so we had to sit in the firelight – if we had sufficient wood – otherwise it meant going to bed. Our worst fears were realised when on January 25th the electricity supply was turned off.

The hewing-down of trees had become more than exercise. The epidemic of indiscriminate attacks with saws and axes on the lovely trees along the St Aubin's road was quite unbelievable; even the gates of St Luke's Church had gone. When the Bailiff visited the scene he was appalled at the despoliation. The Kommandant ordered that the entire wood situation was to come under the control of the Occupying Authorities. With immediate effect all illicit cutting and gathering of wood was forbidden, whether by owners or occupiers of land on which it stood ie in private grounds, farms, parks and roadside. It remained to be seen whether the Germans themselves would adhere to this prohibition.

Further restrictions to our daily existence were published. Most of the telephones were cut off, only essential services being permitted. Butter was excluded from all ration books, and meat would now only be available every other week. Milk for adults was rationed at half a pint four times a week. Fortunately I was still able to collect some milk from my farmer friends, but great care had to be taken. I carried small bottles in socks strapped to my legs as I did not want to be caught with the milk, which very nearly happened on one occasion. A ration of half a pint of paraffin was also available for invalids and mothers with babies.

Churches held a thanksgiving service for the arrival of the Red Cross supplies. It was still difficult to see during the services as electricity was only just coming back in limited use, from 6.15pm to 11.30pm only.

The St John's Ambulance Brigade also held a thanksgiving service on January 14th. They were very fortunate in being allowed to continue functioning and wear uniforms. They had undertaken splendid work throughout the Occupation and of late had helped with the distribution of Red Cross supplies.

The Constable of St Helier warned householders that, as there were no telephones to contact the police, people should raise a noisy alarm if they thought they heard intruders. There had been many robberies over several months and it had become part of our lives. One woman was sentenced to one month in prison for stealing from a Red Cross parcel.

German doctors were greatly disturbed by the health of their troops. Many soldiers were looking extremely ill, and some had collapsed in the street. 'Lights out' was to be an hour earlier and all sport discontinued. But, and this amused us greatly, soldiers must rest in the afternoon (!).

Young Mr de la Haye brought the news that he had seen an American plane shot down over St Brelade's Bay. It had crashed into a minefield. He spotted the pilot who had bailed out, and at once went to the rescue on a float. Unfortunately he was obliged to leave the pilot on a rock as he neared the shore as his float started to break up. He swam ashore for further assistance. A German also went out to help but ran into the same difficulty and landed on the same rock. However, they were eventually both brought ashore.

Stories about secreting food etc abounded. There was one woman who, when the Germans arrived to search the house, quickly got into bed pretending to be very ill. She had half a pig wrapped in a sheet alongside her – quite an interesting bedfellow!

The following is the gist of a message from the Bailiff which appeared in the *Evening Post* on February 2nd. 'The Council in accordance with the German Military Authorities state that the civil bread ration must now be reduced by half. When the representatives of the International Red Cross were here shortly after Christmas, they were accurately informed of the position of our stocks, and were urgently asked to arrange for flour to maintain the civil ration.

> 'Daily we have anxiously awaited news. Unfortunately there is no official news whatever that ships are on the way to us with the stores for which we have asked. If help does not reach us within two weeks the bread ration will cease entirely, in which case a second distribution of food parcels will be delivered later, but this will exhaust our supply. The public must be aware of the gravity of the situation.'

A further message several days later from the Bailiff said that the German Military Authorities had informed him that on the *Vega*'s next visit to the Channel Islands it would bring food parcels for the prisoners of war, but not flour which was so desperately needed. Fortunately for us, along with other folk with extra special needs, Mr Slade again showed his unbounded kindness by supplying us from time to time with a small amount of flour from the portion he had been allowed to retain in previous years as part-payment for the legitimate milling of cereals from local farmers.

From the Field of Honour the sad news came through that Major J. S.Crill had been killed in action. I knew Jack well and also his father, Constable Sidney Crill of St Clement's. The latter had been with me in the Green Room Club production of *Iolanthe* some years ago. He had always been great company.

Friends near Havre-de-Pas swimming pool were highly amused when they saw a squad of Germans collecting limpets in billy cans. Afterwards they lined up with their haul and marched off up Roseville Street into St Helier. I didn't think this would make a very enjoyable meal!

And now another order of impudence! All householders having more than one axe in their possession were obliged to deliver them to the forces against payment at their Parish Hall on February 8th and 9th. Offenders against this order would be punished according to the order protecting the Army of Occupation. Somehow I felt that they would find very few people who had more than one axe: the second would simply have 'disappeared'. I looked forward to the outcome of this order!

However, another order was issued on 28th February, this time addressed to the German Forces:

> 'I have taken over command of the Channel Islands from Graf von Schmettow, who has been called home for reasons of health. I have only one aim: to hold out until final victory. I believe in the mission of our Führer and of our people. I shall serve them with immutable loyalty. Hail our beloved Führer.'
>
> Hueffmeier
>
> Vice-Admiral and Commander of the Channel Islands

The Germans were once more commandeering cycles. A local man was apparently caught while ferreting close to a minefield. His cycle was taken away from him by a soldier who offered to pay him fifty marks (useless money). He was then told that he was trespassing – unlikely in actuality – and would be fined fifty marks. As a result the cheeky soldier rode away with a cycle which cost him absolutely nothing. There was no way in which the poor chap would be able to recover his loss.

One day, when I was outside watching the ducks which had just been let out, the gardener (always known to us as 'Mr Gardener') arrived and said that he and Mr Newland had had a long discussion the night before about the old tree at the bottom of our garden that overhung the hill in a most difficult spot. He would be able to get a couple of friends and some tackle to carefully retrieve it from its perilous position. It was at the far end of the garden where there was a drop of about twenty-five feet into the road below. It would be a total disaster if it fell in that direction, but it was at such an awkward angle for cutting.

I asked 'Mr Gardener' if he and his friends realised the consequences for all of us if we were caught. Yes, they knew it would mean prison. So we decided there and then that, no matter what the consequences, it was now imperative that we cut it down.

A day was decided on when I should be at home. It would be a big undertaking as not only did we have to get the tree down safely into the garden but it would have to be instantly cut up and put away and all traces removed or camouflaged. What happened was a near-disaster.

In spite of all the ropes and tackle, the tree heeled over and caught the electricity wires. You can imagine our horror and utter dismay. Everyone applied themselves to the situation with great urgency. The tree was hauled into the garden and everything possible was done to dispatch the wood in double quick time. The wires caught by the tree led – of all places! – to the house occupied by the troops at the end of the road. Fortunately the tree was well away from the path used by the Germans when they walked through the garden.

Later a soldier arrived at the house and asked about the electricity. Mr Newland replied to his incessant questions that we had no electricity and had been without for some time. This of course was in English but the soldier understood the words 'no electricity'. We felt that this would not be the end of it and that it would soon be traced. However, at last we had some luck for that very evening the troops at the end of the road were all taken away. When replacements arrived the following day, they must have decided that they had been assigned to a place where the electricity supply had been discontinued, like the rest of the neighbourhood. We all felt that this time God was with us.

It was announced that tradesmen were to be subsidised with a grant of

£20,000 to pay their employees on a daily basis of £1 1s 4d per male and 15s for a female, thus enabling them to retain their staff. The few grocery shops remaining open only had the horrible breakfast food/porridge to sell, along with whatever paltry rations were available. But when the *Vega* arrived there was always more to do. This also enabled them to retain their staff, thus keeping them from having to be employed by the Department of Labour.

Following an announcement on the BBC [picked up on an illegal wireless], news flew round the town very quickly that war in Europe would end in a day or two. There was much excitement. People gathered in the streets, little flags appeared on sale and on buildings. All was premature. We were all forgetting that the Germans were still here in occupation, and still on duty at every gun post around the Island, with no intention of capitulating.

The Germans announced the allocation of 1 cwt of wood to people holding a medical permit. Mr Newland would thus be a recipient, for which we were grateful. A certificate had to be countersigned by the German tree inspector. We could apply to cut down a tree but it would mean that we would be obliged to have the tree inspector come here. It was feasible that he might even decide to cut down all our pine trees. And before you knew it, he would be in the house and possibly wanting to take it over, or billet soldiers here. It was not worth the gamble.

The Germans had been felling trees indiscriminately, just going for the easiest available after taking the tools away from civilians and the Department of Labour gangs. The tree inspector thought that he was doing a wonderful job and expected to have large stocks of wood ready for the civilian population by August 1st. I could not believe that he – along with the rest of them – would still be here then, and in any case we needed the wood immediately.

With fuel having become such a real problem for many people, the depredation of trees and shrubs in many areas had become clearly apparent. The old railway station at Greve d'Azette had been completely gutted with doors, cupboards and even the wood floors disappearing. Unattended houses faced the same danger. At this time the main focus of damaged property was the St Helier area, for any houses occupied by German troops would certainly suffer the same fate.

One night, in the latter part of February, hundreds of houses both in the town and in the country had swastikas painted on them with tar. This time it was not done by locals but surprisingly was the work of the German marines, who did the job most systematically. The reason for this dastardly disfiguration was never fathomed. Householders tried hard to paint over the tarred areas but their efforts proved hopeless.

It was learned that the Military Authorities were extremely annoyed about the swastika-painting activities of the marines as it was obvious that they were becoming undisciplined. That was all we needed! After many voluble and irate complaints, men were now working on the removal of the tar. In many cases it was chipped off which meant ruination for the facade of any house. It would certainly cost a lot of money for the property to be made good again. Can you imagine what the householders felt about this disfigurement!

Around this time a number of people were sentenced to prison for possessing crystal sets. Others who had written letters to England which had been lost by hopeful escapees but later found by the Germans were also detained.

We had a new Kommandant, General Wolff, who replaced our so-called 'Fortress Kommandant' who had been transferred to Guernsey. We certainly had a lot of changes – German officialdom! This one might prove to be more difficult. He was already unpopular with his officers as he had made them give up their cars and mess with the men. It was not proving to be a very happy life for them.

The new Kommandant might be made of sterner stuff than his predecessor, but he had at least begun paying for the potatoes and swedes which the farmers had been obliged to supply to the forces. A new order from the Kommandant forbad the cutting of pasture: this was to ensure a good hay crop for fodder – would our cows and horses get some, or would it all go to his horses, I wondered.

In addition, guards were now patrolling fields and glasshouses. They arrested thieves caught during the day, but were authorised to shoot if the thieves tried to escape. At night thieves would be shot without hesitation. This had already been the fate of one non-commissioned officer.

One did not have to be blessed with too much imagination to realise that the German hospitals would soon be overflowing. The Germans had also acquired the Chelsea Hotel in Gloucester Street, using it to keep those arrested who were waiting to go to prison.

We heard that some of the old barges had been broken up for wood. Railway sleepers between Don Bridge and Corbiere disappeared overnight, but I think that the latter may have been stolen by locals. Persons whose identity cards had been taken away for illicit wood-cutting were able to get them back, but the wood was confiscated. Germans had also been taking away tools and handcarts.

Friendship leagues were doing their best to help alleviate the distress experienced by many of the older folk who had not been able to get in reserves of fuel. After six weeks of intense cold the poor folk were now in a pretty poor condition. Nursing homes seldom had a spare bed, which was quite understandable. Soup was being given to children at school every day.

We learned that the Germans had been warned about using sea water for cooking vegetables. Civilians were advised to take note of this as it might result in serious boils. We confined ourselves to rendering the sea water down to obtain the salt, which was of a greyish colour.

It now officially became known that the Germans were having dogs and cats killed and dressed at the slaughterhouse. For some time many residents had been losing their pets.

Butchers were informed by the local authorities that, due to the lack of refrigeration because there was no electricity, meat in store would have to be sold. So instead of a meatless week we would each be able to obtain a ration. This was wonderful news. The local authorities had certainly been on the ball and done some real wangling. I wished that this could have happened more often.

The Germans had not sent the weekly ration of coal, which fired the machinery used for separating the milk, so they missed out on their butter and skimmed-milk rations. It was given out by some German official that the public could buy any amount from the dairy in Don Street (I thought that he must be on our side). Can you imagine the rush from the townspeople? No doubt the official in charge of that department was pretty quickly demoted as only just before this the Germans had been demanding enormous quantities of butter per day, without any proper agreement. Not long afterwards the Bailiff and Attorney-General went to College House in connection with milk supplies. Also in attendance was a most aggressive German and so-called dairy expert, but our people were up to coping with him.

The German military got a bit of a shock on March 23rd when two Union Jacks were seen suspended between the towers of Victoria College. Someone had been active during the night. The flags were immediately taken down and the Acting Headmaster, Mr P.A.Tatam, was questioned. Mr Tatam explained that in the first instance the Germans had never allowed the College grounds to be locked up at night. Secondly, when the troops had occupied the building some time ago they had lost the key to the towers. He then said that a German helmet had been found in one of them (was this a clever stratagem on someone's part?).

This was the second time the College grounds were in the news around that time. Just prior to the Union Jack episode, the grounds had been the scene of a serious fracas between German soldiers and sailors, who fought each other with knives.

The Germans had a bit of luck. Having stolen all the nets from the tennis courts from which they had made fishing nets, they came up with a huge catch of sea-snipe in St Brelade's Bay. Not long after this they held a meeting to inform local fishermen who wanted to fish that they must hand over seventy per cent of their catches. They would be paid the retail price, such as it was, but many of the fishermen refused. I don't blame them for turning down such a paltry offer.

Someone was busy one night as paintings of the Union Jack, French Tricolour and V for Victory signs were all very artistically produced in the town. Like the Germans we were becoming bolder. Some of the children watching the band playing in the Royal Square had been wearing red, white and blue favours under their coats.

On February 19th we were dismayed to see our last supply of a 1lb loaf of bread, but this was to be augmented by an extra ration of potatoes. Sad to say a lot of them were not very good and had to be thrown out. Imagine our disappointment when the *Vega* arrived on its second trip and there was no flour on board. People were greatly distressed at this information but we of course were looking forward to the arrival of the food parcels. We knew that the Germans still had a ration of 4lb of flour per week, and they also held a large

German soldiers and Island residents watch a German band play in the Parade Gardens.
(Photo courtesy Jersey Evening Post).

amount of our wheat. They certainly were not going to release any of their stocks to us. They apparently felt it quite in order to provide for the military at the expense of a starving population. This was not all, for at night they actually organised some robberies at civilian bakeries. It was reported that over three hundred loaves were stolen from the First Tower Bakehouse.

Our friends at Bagatelle had a front-row view of a tremendous fire which broke out at the Palace Hotel where the Germans had been located since the beginning of the Occupation. This was just across the field at the back of their garden. It was followed by a violent explosion when the fire reached what must have been an enormous ammunition dump. This caused tremendous damage in the surrounding area. It was felt for miles around with debris found in all the neighbouring gardens and fields. It had been a lovely hotel.

Later fifteen gasometers blew up and ammunition explosions were continually heard for some time afterwards. I could not envy the fire brigade tackling a job of this dimension. More fires followed at Mount Bingham, a garage at Georgetown and several other garages in St Helier. Could these be sabotage?

Some fishermen who had risked putting down a net had made a good haul, some 800lbs of fish which they were able to barter with and sell to people in their neighbourhood. This was one lot that the Germans were not going to get their hands on. Some time previously, a fisherman with a permit had brought in a good haul of spider crabs at Gorey but the Germans had walked off with practically the lot. However, along St Ouen's Bay the Germans had been busy collecting hundreds of dead squid which had been washed ashore. They were most welcome to this ghastly lot.

The *Vega* again returned on March 10th – her third trip. It was once more unloaded by French colonial troops, who were prisoners of war, and the supplies were checked in at Maitlands store by the St John's Ambulance Brigade: food and diet parcels, cases of soap, flour, sacks of salt, yeast and medical supplies. In addition there was diesel oil to work the cranes and petrol for the ambulances. All this was in the nick of time as many folk were almost on starvation rations.

But best of all was the desperately-needed flour. The Island had a supply of coke which the gasworks had hidden from the Germans, so by the next day loaves were already made. We had seen nothing like them for several years! They were double the size of the loaves we had become used to. We were so very thankful.

Coincidently the following Sunday was Refreshment Sunday in the Church's calendar and the gospel for the day was the story of the feeding of the five thousand! That night the BBC broadcast a service held by Channel Island refugees in Westminster Hall, London. The reception was clear, even on the crystal sets, which was great for those who had them.

An extra bonus from the *Vega*'s arrival were the Red Cross messages, which were distributed. Irene was fortunate to receive one from a friend which simply said, 'All well.'

The new German staff were spreading it around that they were expecting an invasion, and began requisitioning a large number of houses for billeting concentrations of troops in several parts of the Island. They again strengthened defences, particularly around the north and east coasts of the Island. No wonder that we saw so many troops along our road. We lived in constant fear that we would be turned out of our house at any time.

They were also busy looking for poor underfed Russians who made their escape from time to time. There had been a great deal of trouble at the Russian camps.

Being unable to come to an agreement with the Islanders, the Germans now took over the Don Street Dairy and its entire production for their own consumption, forcing Dairy staff to move to other premises. Any time now the inevitable cut in rations would come, thus curtailing supplies to the civilian population. It was just one more restriction to face in our daily lives.

Easter Saturday was the last day of March. The flower trade did extremely good business. Vegetables such as cabbage and cauliflower were now available. A German band played in the Royal Square, attended by General Wolff. Easter Sunday was rather dull and showery, but in spite of that there were good attendances at the churches. Sad to relate, the altar candles at St Andrew's Church were stolen, just one in a long string of robberies.

On April 9th, following the *Vega*'s most recent trip, we received our sixth Red Cross parcel. There were not sufficient parcels to go round, but fortunately there were some left over from the previous consignment. In addition to the parcels from Canada and New Zealand there were special supplies for invalids and a Red Cross tablet of soap for each child under two.

Several medical delegates of the International Red Cross were on board. They had details concerning the evacuation of invalids. The evacuation would be on a voluntary basis: Jersey's quota was 600. The invalids were to be examined by German doctors and a Medical Commission. However, the hospital ship would not be arriving for another six to eight weeks! My father-in-law hoped to be in England by then, and that we should all be free. I hoped he was right.

On April 20th, to celebrate Hitler's birthday, the Germans organised a concert in the Royal Square featuring a band and a choir. Trying to put on a brave show, the Kommandant declared in his address that they would defend the Island until the very end. Rashly he also said that the Russians would never take Berlin.

To say this now showed that he just wasn't facing the reality of the situation. Did he not realise that at St Catherine's breakwater, not far from our home, two 'artillery floats' – a vessel rather like a heavily-armed barge – were fired on by one of our Allied planes. Swooping down, it dropped a bomb on one of them and machine-gunned the other.

Occasionally Allied planes attacked various gun emplacements around the Island. Sometimes there was a little damage to property but in general they were pretty careful in selecting their target. It meant a bit of excitement for all.

In spite of all the difficulties and restrictions, four young Islanders made an attempt to escape from the Island. Their boat was smashed against the cliffs on the north-east side of the Island; sad to say, all four were drowned. However, others were more fortunate and achieved their desired destination.

On April 23rd, St George's Day, many people wore a red rose. We were lucky enough to receive a few extra rations. The bread ration was increased from 1lb to 5lb. This replaced the potato ration, which had been discontinued for the time being. Other rations included canned milk for adults and from the Red Cross 6oz of salt, one candle for everybody, a box of matches and half a tablet of soap. Owing to the lack of fuel, eleven bakehouses and registered restaurants were forced to close, but the communal kitchens would still be able to serve soup.

The farmers continued to have their houses searched for food. The Germans just walked in and opened cupboards to see what they contained. At times they held up householders at point of gun or bayonet. Troops were out in the fields digging up the seed potatoes that had only recently been planted. Those in our garden met with the same fate.

Soldiers could be seen picking nettles from hedges along country lanes, presumably for making soup. Worst of all for the farmers was that they might have to give up more of their land. This would mean that soldiers working in the fields would have to be billeted with them in their homes and share their food. They would be completely deprived of privacy. I really felt for the farmers, subjected as they were to such an unbearable and monstrous ploy.

The latest, almost nightly, occurrence was that soldiers were now shooting and gutting pigs in their sties. Things were becoming more and more horrible.

During the momentous days of April 1945, when the prospect of peace in Europe was within our grasp, we heard the sad news that President Theodore Roosevelt had died. It was such a pity that he was not spared so that he could savour the hard-earned victory of the Allies over the Nazi Regime.

The Red Cross Fund was swelling all the time: it was now over £64,000. We were certainly all agreed: 'Thank God for the Red Cross parcels.' Apart from them, the only rations we had to live on were 7oz of breakfast meal, two pints of milk per week, 4oz of meat per fortnight and, if we were lucky, some vegetables. That was the sum total.

The Turner sisters, who were students of mine, all appeared in my productions. On September 16th 1944, the eldest, Belza, had tried to escape with her Dutch friend in a rubber dinghy which they had removed from one of the ships. Unfortunately it was a failure and after two tortuous days they were swept back onto the rocks at Corbiere instead of arriving at the French coast. I felt very sorry for them. They were both taken to prison where they remained for fourteen weeks until appearing before a court martial, where they were sentenced to imprisonment for the duration of the war. However, happily they were both released in April 1945 and Belza was welcomed back into class, once more able to rehearse her parts in my Liberation revue.

CHAPTER TEN

FINALE

May 1st saw some shops in the town openly selling Union Jacks. People were carrying them around in the street with the Germans looking on. Late that evening came the news of Hitler's death. The Germans were all looking very distressed, but not us. Everyone was now becoming very excited. The Kommandant of the Channel Islands arrived from Guernsey to have meetings with the local officers. Subsequently they issued a notice to their troops not to fire on any planes and to clear the airport of all fortifications. Some of the Gestapo had now gone into uniform to merge with the troops.

A number of incidents were reported of civilians beating up Germans. Such was the excitement that some people had been too premature in raising flags. Activity in my studio had now reached fever pitch. Classes were turned into hard-working rehearsals. I was just praying that my cycle would hold out, with hosepipe now on both front and back wheels. News was flying around that there was an offer of unconditional surrender, following a BBC announcement that war in Europe should end in a day or two.

Everyone was waiting for some official statement. A message came through from the Bailiff, urging the people to keep calm and refrain from any kind of demonstrations. The position was not clear as we were, after all, still occupied by the Germans.

The Bailiff had asked the Germans for various concessions but they had no intention of giving in to any of the urgent requests. Some of the troops were wandering hopelessly around the town like lost sheep with nowhere to go. The banks were busy with people who, hoping that they would never again need them, were paying in their marks. It was quite unbelievable but there was no slacking in the Germans' war effort; they started building new gun emplacements in various parts of the Island, manned by soldiers. At night the searchlights swept the sea. All was turmoil: were they going to start fighting to retain the Island?

An officer committed suicide at College House and another soldier shot himself at the General Hospital. Such happenings were normally kept very quiet, but it was general knowledge that of late there had been several such incidents.

On May 4th we heard more exciting, indeed wonderful news - the wholesale surrender of the German forces in north-west Germany. Some of them said that they were not Nazis. We felt that as each day passed, it would soon be the turn of the German troops on this Island to lay down their arms.

By now preparations for what was to be my last show were well under way, though we were running behind schedule in providing some of the costumes. Programmes were ready for the printers and most arrangements for final stage rehearsals at the Forum Theatre had been made. All I was waiting for was the final date. Each member of the cast was informed that full rehearsals would take place the second day following the signing of the surrender of Jersey. This would give all concerned time to get over the tremendous excitement before tackling a week's hard work to get everything into good shape. It proved to be almost impossible to get everyone together at once so that I was obliged to fit in as many individual rehearsals as possible. Little did I realise at the time that owing to so much excitement and activity it would become far more difficult than I had imagined.

At last the first official statement of our impending release, eagerly awaited by everyone, was issued by the Bailiff on May 8th 1945.

Message to the people of Jersey from the Bailiff

I appeal to you to maintain your calm and dignity in the hours which lie ahead and to refrain from all forms of demonstration.

It is my earnest wish that services should be held in all places of worship in the same manner as services are being held in the United Kingdom and in other parts of the Empire.

I feel that the conclusion of the Prime Minister's speech this afternoon will be the appropriate moment for the hoisting of flags, and I make the strongest appeal to you, in the interests of public order, not to fly flags before that time.

I was present last evening at the release from custody of the majority of the political prisoners and I am doing all in my power to obtain the immediate release of the remainder of them.

I shall make known to you immediately any further developments.

A.M.Coutanche

Bailiff   **May 8th 1945**

The next morning we were all up early. Even my father-in-law who had been resting most mornings appeared to have gained strength and was up and out in the garden looking for the ducks, coming in with two eggs. After breakfast Irene and I went off to the studio as we had planned to work by ourselves for a while. We would be hearing the latest news in the town. We saw the children being sent home from school and news spread quickly that a message from the Bailiff announced that Mr Churchill would be addressing the nation at three o'clock. It would be an historic speech.

When we left the studio, crowds were already making their way to the Royal Square. We made our way home as fast as the old boneshakers could carry us so as to dig out the old wireless which by now was a strange contraption involving a crystal set with telephone receiver attached. We could then all manage to be together to hear Mr Churchill, all the while desperately hoping our set would work. It was a speech that we had all waited so long to hear, and when Mr Churchill uttered the words 'our dear Channel Islands', we were unable to contain ourselves.

After the Prime Minister had spoken, we managed to hear the Bailiff who had hoisted the Union Jack amidst cheering crowds. We rushed out and did the same. He asked everyone to join him in offering thanks to Almighty God for the deliverance of this Island of ours. He went on to say that there would be no further wireless restriction in the home and that the King was to speak at nine o'clock. He concluded with singing the National Anthem. Never was it sung with so much vigour, but unfortunately not from me - I was too filled with emotion. Out in the garden you could hear the lovely sound of the church bells ringing; happiness abounded in our hearts.

On May 9th we were in for more tremendous excitement when HMS *Beagle* rounded Noirmont Point at 10am. Loud cheering was heard from the harbour and all around the bay. However, it took some time before the Bailiff received a message to attend at College House to speak on the phone with Colonel Power, the Officer Commanding the Armed Forces of the Channel Islands, on board ship. Later a message was received from the *Beagle* stating that the presence of the General Commanding the German Forces in Jersey was required on board. The Bailiff, the Attorney-General and the Solicitor-General together with General Wolff, the German Kommandant, and supporting officers boarded a German naval pinnace [small boat]. On reaching the ship they were met by Brigadier Snow, Rear Admiral Stuart and officers of the ship. They were then taken to meet the other representatives to discuss arrangements for the formal surrender of the Island.

Terrific crowds surrounded the harbour and the wildest of cheers went up when a British pinnace came through the pierheads. Two officers landed at the Albert Pier and, as the officers approached the barrier, the police were unable to control the crowd who surged forward and raised the officers shoulder high before carrying them aloft to the Harbour Office. Here they were showered with flowers. The Union Jack was unfurled from an upstairs window. One more tremendous cheer was followed by the National Anthem amidst unrestrained emotion.

A formation of the RAF flew over the Island and later an officer and ten men of the Hampshire Regiment arrived to a wonderful reception. The captain then made a little speech: 'We would have been here long ago, boys, only it would have meant bombing you to Hell, and very few of you would have been here by now. However, I've just seen General Wolff, and I've given him orders [loud cheers]. We are only a small party and there's a much bigger group coming. You've given us a wonderful reception and I hope you'll give the same to them but don't forget we've lots of work to do disarming these people and getting them out of the Island.' Then the National Anthem was sung again and three cheers for the Tommies were raised.

Colonel W.V.A.Robinson MC, who was to be Chief Commanding Officer of the forces in Jersey, made his way directly to the Pomme d'Or which was to be his headquarters. As you may recall, this was where the German naval personnel had been for five years. He addressed the crowd from the balcony after the Union Jack had been hoisted by H.A.Richmond, Harbour Master of Jersey.

The Tommies who had arrived were all wearing a special shoulder flash, a shield surrounded by three leopards. We later learned that they had been preparing for this landing since the previous September but they had not known until the last whether they were going to have to fight for the Island.

In the afternoon much attention was focused on the Royal Square, where the official ceremonies took place, to hear the respective addresses given by the Bailiff and Colonel Robinson. A Royal Artillery Guard of Honour was drawn up facing the Court House. All members of the States were present, complete with the Royal Mace, the Island's most cherished possession. When the flag fluttered out, the Guard of Honour presented arms and the St James Boys' Brigade struck up the National Anthem. With great emotion the Bailiff said: 'At last the moment we have waited for so long has come.'

He went on: 'I have sent a message ratifying our allegiance to His Majesty the King and also to Mr Winston Churchill.' He then read out the first message in five years from Commander-in-Chief Plymouth. Colonel Robinson, who received a great ovation, then addressed the crowd, saying that the days of being told 'I am the Military Commander and I order you' had gone. He praised all the islanders and then appealed to us to allow his troops more elbow room to bring in food, clothing, vitamins and everything else that was so badly needed. At the conclusion of the ceremony the captain of HMS *Beagle* was presented with a solid silver replica of a Jersey milk can by the Bailiff. Afterwards the

Guard of Honour, headed by the St James'
band, marched around the town.

The first Jersey officer to land was someone
I had known, Captain Hugh Le Brocq, who
had left the Island with the Jersey Militia in
1940. The Germans were ordered to start work
immediately clearing the Fort and the quays,
and all of them except for those in hospital
had to vacate the town by nightfall. Arms and
ammunition were to be left in places
indicated, though some of the Germans were
just throwing them out of the window. It was
simply wonderful; we could not get over this
spectacle.

Later so much happened that it is difficult
to know what to write about next. I do know
that the Bailiff went to visit the French colonial
prisoners in the camp; the British prisoners of
war were already released. The people who still
had cameras and films were busy. Some car
and motor cycles that had been hidden away
very soon appeared, which made me wonder
just how long it would be before I could get my
poor car on the road again after its long sleep.
Would the engine still work and would the
tyres still be serviceable?

I must say that the discipline of the
Germans was good. They carried out some
small demolitions and some of their wood
buildings were pulled down for firewood.

Attempts were being made to get the
telephones in St Helier back into service, but
this would most likely take a few more weeks
for those in the country. So many of us were
looking forward to ringing our friends once
again.

Mr H.S. Morrison, the British Home
Secretary, accompanied by Lord Munster,
Parliamentary Under-Secretary, visited the
Island. They paid tribute to the Bailiff and the
States for their work during the Occupation,

His Majesty's Reply

The Bailiff has received the following signal from Admiral Stuart, Naval Officer in Charge, Channel Islands:

I have been requested to inform you that His Majesty the King has received your messages and that they gave him great pleasure and satisfaction.

Mr. Churchill

To the Bailiff of Jersey from the Commander-in-Chief, Plymouth. Following received:

From the Prime Minister to the Bailiff of Jersey—
You should have heard the House of Commons cheer at the news of your liberation. Every good wish.

The Royal Proclamation

We are officially informed that the reading of the Royal Message and Proclamation will take place in the Royal Square on Sunday afternoon, May 13th, at 3 o'clock.

and to the courage and fortitude of the Islanders.

Orders were published for the restoration of sterling on the Island and reichmarks were be exchanged at the rate of 9.36 marks to the pound. Until free circulation was restored, cash withdrawals would be limited to £5 per person per week.

Greetings continued to be sent to the Island. The latest was from the Archbishop of York and two Jerseymen, Lord Justice du Parq and C.T. le Quesne KC. Free postcards courtesy of the Post Office in London and many English newspapers were distributed. Soon there would be a regular postal service once again, to which we were all looking forward.

The German sailors, still in their boats in the harbour, did not look too happy. At 'La Preference' estate at St Martin's a number of German troops were holding out with machine guns but it took no time at all to dislodge them.

The Military Authorities announced that permits to travel to England would only be available in exceptional cases, most likely in May. It was a great relief for us that at last Mr Newland would soon be able to leave the Island for treatment.

The shop windows all looked so wonderful. Many of the goods were to be made available to the public in the next few days. Around this time there was a distribution of free gifts by the British Government and it was now possible to apply for the return of our cameras and wireless sets. A grant of £2 was made to each child already in receipt of an allowance for the purpose of purchasing clothing. There was a great rush for oranges which went on sale on ration, 1½ lb per person.

The Department of Health advised innoculation against diptheria, especially for children. Many of the German troops had suffered from this during the Occupation.

Islanders were warned about German demolition of the fortifications and were asked to keep the roads clear for the movement of troop transport as much military gear had to be removed. There was an appeal for the public to maintain order as mob law was not consistent with Island traditions.

There were some incidents involving 'Jerry bags', collaborators and black marketeers. A few regrettable scenes had taken place where one or two of the women had been severely handled; troops had been obliged to intervene, otherwise the women might have been killed.

Supplies of British currency amounting to about three-quarters of a million pounds arrived. However, various officials connected with civil affairs had been interviewing bank managers. I imagined that there would be quite a bit of sorting out of all money matters - German currency, Occupation money and the new Jersey banknotes which were printed at that time. There was also what the Germans had commandeered from the bank. A financial review of the situation was presented by Jurat Dorey, magistrate, who pointed out that the public deficit was now over five million pounds!

We were informed that the German garrison in the Channel Islands numbered between 27,000 and 30,000 men. For its size it was one of the most strongly-fortified places in the world. Most of the Germans were now being taken away, and only about a thousand were retained to clear up the mines. Two of them had already been killed carrying out this dangerous task.

May 12th was a gala day. Nobody had to work and there was something to thrill the crowds every minute. A convoy of over fifty ships arrived with the Channel Island pilots on board. We spotted, well to the fore, our Great Western Railway cross-channel steamer SS *St Helier* which was bringing part of the headquarters staff. The greatest attraction of its arrival was the sight of the soldiers and sailors disembarking from amphibian landing craft known at that time as 'ducks'. We had never seen such a form of transport. Tank landing craft came right up to the sea wall at St Aubin's Bay and discharged all kinds of vehicles.

The enthusiasm of the onlookers was so great that even the Germans cleaning up nearby applauded. The first ashore was Commander T. le B. Pirouet RNR who was in charge of landing operations. More and more men including several Jerseymen arrived showering chocolates, sweets and cigarettes on newly-made friends. Constant admiration and brouhaha continued the whole day through.

In the afternoon an historic ceremony took place in the Royal Square on a specially constructed dais. Brigadier A.E. Snow, Military Commander of the Channel Islands, read a proclamation. This was followed by a message from the King 'To the loyal people of the Channel Islands'. It was a moving celebration. The Band of the Duke of Cornwall's Light Infantry and a Guard of Honour by the Royal Marines and men of the Hampshire Regiment were all in attendance.

May 14th, the day of the opening performance of our Liberation revue, *Happy Release*, was fraught with difficulty. I was busy at the Forum going over everything with my stage manager, attempting to put things right in terms of the scene changes, and what curtains had to be pulled where and when. I also needed to see the chief electrician about lighting changes which had not been correct. The fact that we had only been able to have one run-through on stage was really quite a worry. Delays between items was something I certainly could do without.

I was becoming so nervous and tired that when Irene arrived with a flask of tea and sandwiches, she found me resting in the dressing room. After this light refreshment, we then started to make the final check in all the dressing rooms to see if all the costumes had arrived.

The departure of the German officers on the Princess Charlotte was watched by very few.
(Photo courtesy Jersey Evening Post).

Then we had a terrible shock. Irene discovered that we were still two short for one of the dances. Of course, we had no car but fortunately just after we had asked one of the stage hands who had arrived on his cycle to go over to Madame Blondeau, the missing dresses turned up. The cast was now arriving. There was much excitement in the dressing rooms. We had one or two new students who would be with us for the first time and were being helped with make-up.

The show was to begin at 7.30pm and I was ready for the opening number. After the half-hour call was made I went round the dressing rooms to wish everyone good luck. To my horror, on reaching the boys' room I discovered that two of the boys had not yet arrived. They were both in the opening nautical scene and were to make their entrance from the auditorium. There was nothing

BUCKINGHAM PALACE

To my most loyal people in the Channel Islands, I send my heartfelt greetings.

Ever since my armed forces had to be withdrawn, you have, I know, looked forward with the same confidence as I have to the time of deliverance. We have never been divided in spirit. Our hopes and fears, anxieties and determination have been the same, and we have been bound together by an unshakable conviction that the day would come when the islands, the oldest possession of the Crown, would be liberated from enemy occupation. That day has now come and, with all my Peoples, I cordially welcome you on your restoration to freedom and to your rightful place with the free nations of the world.

Channel Islanders in their thousands are fighting in my service for the cause of civilisation with their traditional loyalty, courage and devotion. Their task is not yet ended ; but for you a new task begins at once—to re-build the fortunes of your beautiful Islands in anticipation of reunion with relatives, friends and neighbours who have been parted from you by the circumstances of war. In this task you can count on the fullest support of my Government.

It is my desire that your ancient privileges and institutions should be maintained and that you should resume as soon as possible your accustomed system of government. Meantime, the immediate situation requires that responsibility for the safety of the islands and the well-being of the inhabitants should rest upon the Commander of the Armed Forces stationed in the Islands. I feel confident that the Civil Authorities, who have carried so heavy a burden during the past years, will gladly co-operate with him in maintaining good government and securing the distribution of the supplies which he is bringing with him.

It is my earnest hope that the Islands, reinstated in their ancestral relationship to the Crown, will soon regain their former happiness and prosperity,

(Signed) GEORGE. R. I.

that could be done, no means of making contact at all. I could already hear the orchestra tuning up under the baton of Miss Maude Glendewar, who directed them superbly. The sound of the overture always thrilled me with anticipation of what was to follow.

In the end the boys made it in the nick of time and, in spite of everything, *Happy Release* went off quite well. It needed speeding up because of lack of stage rehearsals, but the following performances met my expectations. The red, white and blue fabric which had been saved since the beginning of the Occupation was very much in evidence in the costumes representing the Allied Forces. I was able to interpolate three of the most popular items from previous revues but one scene which added greatly to the amusement of everyone involved inviting people onto the stage to learn a new dance. Some of the girls also went down into the audience to find partners to dance with them in the aisles to a type of 'Lambeth Walk' routine. For this I had actually written the words and music.

The very patriotic British finale was highlighted by the singing of 'Rose of England', the final speech from Noel Coward's *Cavalcade* and the emotional rendition of the National Anthem, being sung on stage for the first time in five years. The applause was stupendous. During the entire week of performances we received masses of compliments, including words of congratulation from the manager of the Ivor Novello musicals and war correspondent H.C. Shephard, as well as people I did not know including various members of the Forces. Brigadier Snow invited Irene and myself up to Government House as a mark of appreciation. Later on we were very happy to hand over the sizeable profits to the British Red Cross.

After the last night's performance we held a party in the Forum, arranged by friends and some of the cast. Various members of the Forces also joined the gathering. Everyone was happy and enjoyed it all, but for Irene and myself it was also a little sad. We had lived through this Occupation with a closeness to all these young people, but now it was over. We would soon have to say goodbye and turn the page to the next chapter.

At a later date, Irene and I were invited to appear in a concert at the Forum, along with one of the military bands. This was quite a thrill not only for us but also for some of our students as we performed a couple of items from *Happy Release*. More invitations to appear with the troop shows came later but we were obliged to refuse as we hoped to be able to leave the Island as soon as our permits were granted. Then would begin the next chapter of our lives.

The appearance at the Forum was for me quite a highlight of the Liberation days, but this was topped by the visit of King George VI and Queen Elizabeth. On June 7th, after twenty-four hours' delay owing to unfavourable weather, our Royal visitors arrived. Everywhere there was tremendous, jubilant rejoicing. Their Majesties came ashore from HMS *Jamaica* and were met at the Albert Pier by Island and military officials. After a short tour they returned to the States and replied to a local address, before going to Government House for lunch. Afterwards they drove to the airport to board a plane for their visit to Guernsey. It had been a beautiful day and everywhere there were masses of happy people enjoying the Royal progress. We felt we were truly restored once again to the United Kingdom of Great Britain and Northern Ireland after five long difficult years.

EPILOGUE

Here we were at last in a plane winging our way to Southampton. It was hard to believe that our new life was starting. What was in store for me? Where would we live? Would this be the start of a happy and successful future? It was really quite frightening and yet exciting. First of all we were to spend two days in Southampton before going on to London to stay with Irene's aunt and uncle. Unfortunately they lived in Woolwich, rather too far out for us. We tramped the streets of London looking for a place to live and followed every possible lead without success. On the fourth day we sat in Hyde Park dead tired. Over a cup of tea we studied the map and decided we should try further out as long as it was near a tube station. Closing her eyes Irene put her finger on the spot - Putney Bridge Station. OK. We set off for the train and departed, full of hope.

Just outside the station there was a house agent. Again there was nothing for us. However, as we were going out of the door, he called us back and suggested he would try to contact someone else and asked us to return in half an hour. He must have summed us up as being 'the right type' as it turned out to be at his mother's home. It was quite a nice flat at the top of the house with large furnished rooms but with no separate bathroom. We would of course have the use of hers twice a week. Two days later we moved in. Thank God we had a place at last.

I could hardly wait to use the letter of introduction which had been in my pocket all these days. The next day I had my long-awaited interview with Madame Marie Rambert, head of the famous ballet company. She was a very stern and exacting lady, and asked many searching questions. I was beginning to think that this venture of mine was not going to succeed. When finally the conversation was terminated and I thanked her for seeing me, quite out of the blue she said, 'Be at class tomorrow morning at 9.30am.' I could have done a jete across the studio right away - I was so thrilled and excited to be accepted.

The weeks ahead were difficult. I attended classes twice a day, sometimes with her daughter Angela, a very good teacher, strict just like her mother, and sometimes with a Russian lady. Madame was frequently away with her company on tour, but when they were back in town, she would pay us surprise visits to view our progress and occasionally take our class. I was always nervous when she was there.

One day after class the Russian teacher came over to me to say that Madame wished to speak with me. She told me at once that I should relax when I was dancing as I was too tense. And then much to my surprise and delight she suggested that I should attend the company classes when they would be in town the following week. It was a great experience as I was also able to watch their rehearsals. After I had been there for two months, she called me in again and said that she had arranged for me to attend an audition for *The Song of Norway*, being presented by Emile Littler, one of the big names in the business. Robert Helpman was doing the choreography for the concerto ballet and Pauline Grant the folk dances. I was ecstatic when I was chosen to join the large cast, which included many Sadler's Wells singers. I was soon given two understudy roles which added nicely to my salary as a member of the corps de ballet. It was a wonderful production with Grieg's inspiring music. I was truly in my element, and the operetta had a long run at the Palace Theatre, London.

Irene's parents had arrived in England three weeks before us so that Mr Newland could receive urgent treatment in hospital. Although still looking painfully thin having lost seven stone in weight, he seemed to be showing signs of a slight improvement. As yet the Newlands could make no plans for their future until Mr Newland became much stronger.

Life for me now became very busy. I started doing choreography for television musicals, and working with top producers on productions such as *A Midsummer Night's Dream* and *The Tempest* with Robert Atkins in Regents Park. This was followed by film work. Other appointments came my way. I was still dancing and attending class at Rambert's when possible and was always made welcome there. Choreography was really my main interest. After five busy years in London I was enticed to Hollywood where I spent the rest of my career. But that's another story . . . .

STUDENTS WHO APPEARED IN
DONALD P. JOURNEAUX PRODUCTIONS

Christine Ahier
A. Anguitil
F. Aubin
J. Bacon
Thelma Balston
N. Baudains
Beryl Bertram
M. Beuzeval
Barbara Bisson
Kenneth Bisson
S. Bisson
Cecile Blacklin
S. Blanchard
J. Bouchere
B. Brown
Mary Burger
D. Butel

Christine Carter
Walter Catlinet
B. Chall
B. Clark
M. Clark
Pauline Cleworth
Patricia Cole
Stanley Corfield
B. Coutanche

Bernice De Castro
B. De Feu
Mollie de la Mare
Vivienne de la Mare
Douglas Downer

K. Duckworth
Norma Dunn
Thora Dunn

Barbara Elliott
B. Evans

B. Feeney

R. Fox

G. Gallichan
P. Gavey
E. Glendewar
S. Gorval
Joan Gray
Edith Gruchy

Iris Hacquoil
J. Hall
Marcella Hamon
Beryl Hanning
Eric Harrison
Mollie Hawkins
John Hibbs
Joy Hibbs
Beryl Hodgeson
M. Holly
Beryl Huson

Yvonne Illien

Mimi Jackson
Mattie Jezequel
C. Jones
B. Journeaux

Y. Keenan

J. Larkworthy
M. Lechery
J. Lewis
Doreen Le Breton
M. Le Boustillier
B. Le Breuilly
Y. Le Brocq
M. Le Chevre
Phyllis Le Fondre
Jack Le Gresley
Beryl Le Gros
Bill Le Gros

Graham Le Maitre
Kathleen Le Maitre
P. Le Marquand
H. Le Masurier
Monica Le Luesne
Dorothy Le Seelleur
Ezme Le Seelleur
Joan Le Seelleur
John Le Sueur
June Le Sueur
Doreen Lucas

Violet Macfarling
Lorna Mackintosh
Peggy Maine
Graham Mauger
Sonia Mauger
Phyllis Merhet
Lynn Moisin
C. Moon
D. Morley
P. Mulholland

R. Newton
G. Noel
Sally Noel
J. Norman
Joan Norris

B. Ogier
J. Ogier
M. Osborn
R. Osmont

Beryl Picot
Joan Picot
Madge Picot
Joan Prest
Yvonne Proceida
B. Quarry

M. Raynel

GUEST ARTISTS WHO APPEARED IN DONALD P. JOURNEAUX PRODUCTIONS

J. Richardson
E. Ricket
Ivor Rive
J. Robins
D. Romeril
Joyce Romeril
Phyllis Rowden
Mavis Ruff

Dorothy Saunders
R. Sauvey

Beryl Scriven
B. Seear
Mazel Slade
Sefton Smith
B. Soyer
Gillian Stevenson
Nancy Stopher
A. Symonds
Bert Symonds
E. Symonds
Myrtle Syvret

Cyril Tanguy
Doreen Tanguy
Edith Tardivel
Christine Tarr
Harold Taylor
Roy Thomas
J. Thuillier
T. Thuillier
Belza Turner
Edith Turner
Violet Turner

Peter Valpy
Betty Vasselin
A. Vautier
Joan Vautier
Norma Vautier

Barbara Whelan
Ronald Woods

Winnie Arnold
Oscar Aubin
Nellie Binet
Mavis Burton
Arthur Carter
Harold Cabot
Walter d'Alcorn
Bernard Durand
R. Elliott
Tim Feltham
Betty Fielding
Donald Geary
Winnie Halls
Bert Hibbs
Frank Hanning
B. Le Boutillier
Eric Le Conte
Walter Le Gros
G. May
William Perchard
Edna Powell
Selwyn Rowley
Jessie Young
Winnie Young

GLOSSARY

The States of Jersey	The Island Parliament which comprises 12 Jurats, 12 Rectors, 12 Constables, and 17 Deputies.
Bailiff	Chief Magistrate of the five islands and President of the Royal Court and the States of Jersey.
Jurats	Honorary elected judges who together with the Bailiff form the Royal Court. There are twelve Jurats.
Constable	The chief civic head of each parish; the Constable represents his parish in the States. He presides over the Parish Assembly and is head of the Parish police. There is no similarity between the role of a Constable in Jersey and that of a constable in England.
Deputies	Elected representatives who may be said to be the Jersey equivalent of Members of Parliament in the U.K.
The Battle of Flowers	A traditional Jersey event since 1902 when the first Battle of Flowers commemorated the coronation of Edward VIII. The 'battle' is a parade of flower-bedecked floats which takes place on the first Thursday of August each year.

FURTHER READING

A History of the Channel Islands, Raoul Lempriere (Robert Hale & Co)

Lest we forget, Roy Thomas (La Haule Books)

The Nature of Jersey, Philip Le Brocq (Amanuensis Books)

Old Jersey Houses, Joan Stephens (Commercial Art Company, Jersey)